ELVIS-STRAIGHT UP

By Joe Esposito & Joe Russo

Elvis-Straight Up

Published by Steamroller Publishing, LLC

www.elvisstraightup.com

Book & Cover Design by Joe Russo and Lauren McMullen and The Dream Factory

© Copyright 2007 Steamroller Publishing, LLC
All rights reserved. No part of this book may be reproduced or transmitted in any form or by any means, electronic or mechanical, including photocopying, recording, or by any information storage and retrieval system, without the written permission of the Publisher, except where permitted by law. For information write to:
info@steamrollerpublishing.com

Steamroller Publishing books may be purchased for
business or promotional use or for special sales.
For more information please write to: info@steamrollerpublishing.com

ISBN: 978-0-9797132-0-0

I would like to thank the following ladies and gentlemen who have aided, abetted and/or enhanced my appreciation of Elvis Presley, many whom have contributed to this book:

Steve Barile & Family, Tom Baittie, Bill Bram, The Tunzi Family, Claude Baker, Bil & Laura Baker, Chuck Farrell, Gene Dinapoli, Patsy Andersen, Sherif Hanna, Keith & Marsha Alverson, Tom & Marge Fossa, Brian Bitchachi, Mike Pagliuca, Megan Murphy, Andy Klein, Bob Klein, Jim Hannaford, Tanya Watson, Tim Healy, Sam Thompson, Andrew Hearn, George and Dean Nichopoulos, Nancy Sinatra, Lou Fanty, Helmut Rauch, Harold Newton, David Hamal, Lauren McMullen & The Dream Factory, Daniel Lombardy and especially Joe Esposito for the privileged opportunity to help tell his story.
-Joe Russo

Photo Credits:
Photofest, Starfile, Steve Barile/Joe Russo photo archives, Phil Gelormine (page 87), Sherif Hanna (page 82), Keith Alverson (back cover)

JOE ESPOSITO spent nearly twenty years as Elvis's road manager, confidant, and close friend. Joe helps set the record straight about Presley's private life and career, dispelling the innumerable lies, half-truths and rumors that have evolved over the years. (for more information, please visit the official Joe Esposito site at www.tcbjoe.com)

JOE RUSSO is a published author, songwriter and performer. He has been an Elvis fan since seeing Presley live as a young boy in 1972, during Elvis's legendary stint at New York's Madison Square Garden. He has contributed to numerous Elvis-related projects over the years, and his 17 year experience as an entertainer lends itself to his insights as a "rock n' roll writer". This is his fourth book.

FEATURING

INTRODUCTION / WHY ME? 1

ELVIS & "THE BOOK" 9

ELVIS & TURNING FORTY 21

ELVIS & "PRESLEY CENTER COURTS" 25

ELVIS & DR. NICK 29

ELVIS & THE COLONEL 39

ELVIS & HIS MUSIC 51

ELVIS & HIS FANS 59

ELVIS & PRISCILLA 67

ELVIS & LINDA THOMPSON 81

THE DAY THE MUSIC DIED 91

ELVIS & THE IMAGE.. 99

ELVIS & RECORDING & GINGER ALDEN 107

Elvis-Straight Up

Introduction

WHY ME?

I first met Elvis Presley in the Army in August 1959 and began working for him soon after we were both released from the service in 1960. Literally, until the day he died seventeen years later, my life circled around his, and the incredibly bizarre and exciting world he lived within became my existence as well. It was a wild, crazy ride. And despite some very tense periods, I loved every minute of it!

For over thirty years, I have been asked by people of all ages from all over the world countless questions about him. There doesn't seem to be one detail about the man that people *aren't* interested in. Over the years, I have always tried to be as forthright with my answers as I can. There's no question Elvis was a highly unique and gifted individual. But he was a person too. During the years immediately after his death, I grappled over how to answer some of the more difficult questions being asked about Elvis's life, and I came to the decision that telling the truth in as thoughtful a way as I can works best.

You have to realize, I was with Elvis for seventeen years. That's a long time. And being with Elvis was no nine-to-five job, believe me. Elvis's demanding lifestyle meant you had to be available twenty-four hours a day, seven days a week. He was a handful, and you never knew from one day to the next what adventure he would call upon us to explore with him, or what insane lengths we might have to go to fulfill one of his outlandish desires or elaborate requests.

So much was happening so fast during those years. Elvis was always so on the go that it's sometimes hard to pair events with the eras in which they took place. I have tried in the past to assemble my memories into a book, but it really is an unrealistic expectation. How could I possibly squeeze seventeen years of experiences with Elvis Presley into two or three hundred pages? Well, I'll tell you...you can't. It would take a hundred books to even come close. It may sound crazy, but that's the dilemma that inspired this "Elvis-Straight Up" series. Now, I'm not promising we're going to literally do a hundred books, but a series affords a lot more freedom to elaborate on a wider variety of stories, and in far greater detail than ever before.

I am thrilled to be working with noted writer and Elvis historian, Joe Russo, as my collaborator. Joe possesses an uncanny ability to recapture the thrill and intensity of living with Elvis almost as vividly as when it actually happened. Being involved in the entertainment field himself has afforded him incredible insight into the business and the personalities involved. He has been helping me unjar the details of those years with Elvis from my aging memory so we can put them out there for fans all over the world to enjoy.

Joe Russo's requisite for the book, and I thoroughly agreed with him, was that this project have no agenda other than telling the plain truth. No axe to grind. No ulterior motive. No score to settle. I was not to relieve myself from accountability, and I was not to absolve Elvis from his. What is told here is what really happened, for better or worse. I held nothing back this time and trusted Russo's talent, objectivity and compassion to do the rest. What we have created here is, I believe, the most balanced, thoughtful and heartfelt account of life with Elvis Presley I, or anyone, is likely ever to produce.

I'd like to start by giving you a thumbnail description of what I believe "Elvis Presley" was made of.

First, I'd like to make one thing very clear. Elvis Presley possessed a very special magic and power, not only as a performer, but as a human being as well.

As a performer, there simply has never been any equal. That may sound like an extreme statement, but I am convinced it's true. Sure, there have been dozens, perhaps hundreds, of legendary singers and entertainers throughout history, all of them unique and important in their own way. But Elvis Presley's talent came from another place. Nobody has what he had. It's that simple. It was reserved only for him. He was the only entertainer in the world, and I have had the privilege to know and observe many of the greats, who could move and inspire people, all kinds of people, to the level he could. Once he "touched" you, that was it. You were hooked for life.

And as a human being? As long as I live, I know I will never see anyone have such a profound effect on people. He could make anyone, and I mean anyone, feel like he or she were the most important person in the world just by talking with them. He had charisma and charm that is just indescribable. And do you know something? He didn't even *have* to sing! When Elvis entered a room, even if you didn't see him come in, you could feel the energy of his presence tingle at your nerves because the power of his magnetism was that intense.

Trust me. Elvis was just as perplexed by this phenomenon as you or I are today. For the most part, he was a very humble man. But he was keenly aware of his unique gifts and spent most of his life searching the realms of spirituality for clues as to why *he* was chosen to be "Elvis Presley". Over and over throughout his life he asked himself, "Why me?"

To be honest, in the years since his death, I have thought about my life with Elvis and have asked myself the same question, "Why *me*?"

Before I met Elvis, I was a kid from a nice little Italian neighborhood in Chicago. Except for one trip to Montana, I never traveled anywhere. The last place I'd ever have thought to visit on my own would have been Memphis, Tennessee. Why, of all the people Elvis met in the service, did he pay special attention to me? In fact, *why* was I even *in* the Army? It wasn't until after my discharge that I was informed I was exempt all along and shouldn't have been there in the first place! That was pretty amazing happenstance, don't you think? Did destiny lead me into the Army for the sole purpose of meeting Elvis Presley? Why was I selected to become "right hand man" to one of the most celebrated and influential personalities in history? To see and do things in life that my friends and family back home could only dream of. To be chosen by Elvis Presley as a best man at his wedding, for Chrissake?

It must have been that mysterious phenomenon known as fate. The whole situation was just too farfetched to be anything else. I can't explain it, but I know I am eternally grateful for it.

Not that I would or could ever forget him, but Elvis's immortality and enduring popularity all over the world assures me a day will never go by without me thinking of him in some way.

If even a small notion of how larger than life Elvis was, or how incredible a time I had being with him is conveyed to the reader by the stories and memories in these books, it will bring me one step closer to answering that question I mentioned earlier for myself…"Why me?"

ELVIS & "THE BOOK"

Weeks prior to Elvis's death in August of 1977, a paperback book titled *Elvis, What Happened?* was released by Random House publishers. It was authored by a tabloid journalist named Steve Dunleavy based on interviews with former fellow "Memphis Mafia" members Red West, his younger cousin Sonny West and one of Elvis's karate instructors, Dave Hebler. The three bodyguards were unceremoniously fired in mid-1976, but instead of lying low until the situation resolved itself, they made a terrible, drastic decision that shattered Elvis's world and created the greatest devastating upheaval in his personal life since the passing of his beloved mother.

The book would become a blockbuster, one of the best-selling paperbacks of all time. It's timing couldn't have been better, or worse, depending on which end of the gun barrel you were on.

Red West and Elvis were very, very close. They were from the same part of Memphis and went to the same school together. The incident that cemented them forever happened during their days

at Humes High School, when Red thwarted a group of bullies from beating up on Elvis. From then on, they were thick as thieves. Red eventually took on the role of protecting Elvis with his life until the day they parted company, over twenty years later. Red was there from the beginning, his sincerity proven by the fact that he befriended Elvis long before he was a star. Red was one of the few members in the "Memphis Mafia" who knew his mother, Gladys. Elvis and Red were very tight. There's no question about it. In a way, they were brothers. They loved like brothers, and on more than one occasion, they clashed like brothers.

Personally, I had no problem with Red. In those days we all basically put aside whatever personality differences we may have had with one another for the sake of getting along and enjoying the exclusive bond we shared as members of Elvis's entourage. Actually, Red had some showbiz talents of his own. At the time he was gaining exposure as a stuntman, actor, and later, acting coach (He eventually opened his own school.), a field he has excelled in over the years. Red was also an unlikely but very apt songwriter. He wrote some very fine tunes that Elvis recorded including "If You Think I Don't Need You", "Separate Ways", "If Every Day Was Like Christmas" and "Seeing Is Believing". Red was somewhat of a paradox; tough as nails but with the heart of a poet. To the outside world, he was tough. But he had to be in order to shoulder the responsibilities he had to shoulder for Elvis. And let's face it, if he hadn't kicked the hell out of those bullies that day at Humes, he might never have bonded with Elvis the way he had in the first place! Overall, I would say Red was a good guy during the years I worked with him, despite his short fuse.

The first time I became aware of this "short fuse" of his was the day I met him in Bad Nauheim, Germany, near where Elvis and I were stationed in the Army. Elvis flew him over from Memphis to be around and have fun with during his time off duty. I was sitting at a table in the local pub talking with some of my fellow servicemen when all of a sudden this fight breaks out behind me. Before I knew what was happening, Red West is beatin' the hell out of some guy at the bar. To this day, I don't know what that poor guy said or did, but Red knocked the hell out of him!

Perhaps it was an omen. Red eventually had to return home to Memphis. One of the factors being because the Army was giving him hell about the skirmishes he was having with the locals. Ironically, history would repeat itself about seventeen years later when Elvis's father, Vernon, actually fired Red and his cousin, Sonny, claiming it was because of some costly lawsuits leveled against Elvis that involved fights they had instigated.

Now, every one of us who had ever worked for Elvis had been fired at *least* once. It was something that was inevitable if you were around him for any period of time. But we also knew, one way or the other, sooner or later you would be asked to come back. So for the life of me I could never understand, until this day, why Red and Sonny turned against Elvis the way they did. Scorned, they retaliated by aligning themselves with a sensationalist writer and began work on an explosive "tell all" expose of Elvis's personal life, his faults, bad habits and temper tantrums. To be fair, they also covered a lot of the good times as well: Elvis's generosity, his immense talent, his love affair with his fans, etc. The main purpose of the book however, was to return fire and blow the lid off the Presley myth. But why was this even happening? Didn't they realize their being fired was likely only temporary? They were let go in July of 1976, and within six months we were reading sample chapters of this book eventually known as *Elvis, What Happened?*

Well, I'll tell you "what happened". As Elvis poured over the pages, reading the most salacious things he could ever imagine anyone saying about him, he became ashen. He was devastated. He was convinced this book would destroy his whole life. And in a way, I really believe it did.

After the contents of that book were revealed to Elvis, I believe a large part of his spirit just gave up. He lost his will to fight. On-stage, he was always singing the lyric, "Lord, this time you gave me a mountain...I may never climb." Although I never voiced my fears to a soul at the time, inside, I had a terrible feeling this might be that mountain. The book did not *literally* kill Elvis of course, but its arrival came at a point in his life when its impact was greater than his damaged spirit could bear. I knew one thing -- we were all in for some very troubled times.

You have to put the situation in proper perspective to fully appreciate the devastating effect the thought of this book coming out had on Elvis's psyche. He already had enough problems. His hospitalizations, weight struggles and his drug dependency were taking their toll. He was stigmatized with his age ever since he turned forty a year and a half earlier. He had just split with Linda Thompson, a decision that saddened all of us and was probably one of the biggest mistakes of his adult life. He was also highly stressed over his relationship with Ginger Alden, a young girl he was infatuated with, and it was frustrating the hell out of him;

and now *this*. It destroyed his self-esteem and crushed his spirit.

You must also consider the fact that this incident occurred at a time when a scandal such as this would destroy an entertainer's career, not enhance it like it would today. Today, celebrities blow the whistle on *themselves* for the media attention and free publicity such controversy generates for them.

But at the time, it had Elvis pretty well convinced it would bring an end to everything he worked all his life to achieve. Immediately and with "condition red" intensity, he became obsessed with the book -- completely obsessed. He would rant incessantly for hours every night, sweating over the multi-faceted threat it posed. It tortured his conscience. One major concern was the damage he feared it would cause to his relationship with his young daughter, Lisa Marie, once she was old enough to read it. Elvis would become incensed by anything that threatened the welfare of his daughter, whatever it was. The embarrassment and humiliation he knew the book's sordid details would create for himself, his family, his fans and for all of us, gnawed at him. He desperately feared the shy, humble, clean-living country boy persona he and the Colonel had cultivated so successfully for two decades would be shattered into millions of pieces overnight.

More that anything, it hurt him that his own guys were behind it -- people he knew for so long and trusted so completely; not so much Hebler, who was a relative newcomer, but with Sonny and especially Red. Elvis just couldn't get over it. It was the last thing he thought would ever come from members of his inner circle. It was a cardinal rule among us never to discuss Elvis's personal life with anyone, especially the press. Estrangement or not, it was absolutely beyond his comprehension they would try to do such harm to him -- and with the tabloids, no less!

In defense of Red and Sonny, they were dealt a heavy blow. They lived for Elvis. They put their lives on the line many times to protect him. They were fired with virtually no financial safety net, Sonny particularly took a freefall into some pretty hard times. What was really nothing more than just a bad judgment call was allowed to escalate into a tragedy. Everyone made the wrong decisions. Vernon should not have fired them in such an inconsiderate and unsympathetic manner, and the guys should never have taken such extreme, irreversible retaliation. But stubbornness, the male ego and plenty of testosterone were making a shambles of just about everything. Vernon, who always resented the Wests to begin with, unwittingly set his own son up for disaster and opened him up to attack.

I have seen Elvis angry, broken up, and devastated with sorrow, but this incident had him on the tiles. His biggest fear was the loss of his audience. He feared the shocking revelations of his troubled personal life would destroy their adoration and respect for him. Just the thought of such a possibility literally tore him apart inside.

I knew one thing for certain: Elvis without the love and support of his fans was a dead man. He lived for his fans. They kept him going. Psychologically, he associated the book with the loss of his public. No public...no Elvis.

While we're on the subject, don't think for a second that by admitting Elvis was having a tough time that last year of his life,

that I support any of the ludicrous allegations that Elvis committed suicide. Elvis would never have stopped being "Elvis Presley" as long as the people wanted him. He never, ever would have done such a thing under any circumstances, and I'd stake my life and my reputation on that statement. Suicide, especially in the manner alleged, goes against everything Elvis believed in and stood for. Please, whatever you hear, never believe a word of this utter nonsense. It is nothing more than a concocted, sensational fantasy designed to sell books, or perhaps even a motion picture.

Anyway, we did what we could to have the book stopped, but they said it was too late. Elvis tried to fool himself into believing it would never actually come out, and he lived in denial for a while. But once we got the advance chapters, and Elvis realized he was going to have to deal with it, the stress it created had an immediate impact on his self-image and his physical appearance.

In late 1976 when Elvis became aware of the book's development, he went on a massive weight loss program hoping his improved physical appearance would quell any potential rumors spawned by gossip about the book. Elvis had slimmed down and was looking and performing amazingly well. He had given some of the best shows I'd seen him do for a long time on our final tour in December that year. But as details about the book mounted and he realized the book was a reality and its release was imminent, he fell into a deep, miserable funk, got "out of it" and started his self-destructive binging. In no time, he undid all that hard work and before you knew it, he was looking real heavy again. From that point on, life became a constant struggle to keep his mind off the book, trying instead to convince him he could fend off whatever blows the book dealt by getting himself back into shape and putting on some ultra-fine shows to prove to the world he still had it. But the fuse was already lit.

And as we know, Elvis's next scheduled tour following the book's release would never happen.

I heard Red has regrets today about doing the book, and I believe he does. I know it sounds strange, but I'm certain it had to hurt him tremendously not to be able to attend Elvis's funeral. Like I said, they fought like brothers, but they loved like brothers also.

Red also claims Dunleavy played up the negative angles and omitted a lot of the positive material from the released manuscript. That may be so, but that doesn't change the nightmares it caused us in 1977. Ironically, the book ultimately did not have the effect Elvis feared. His fans did not abandon him. They never have. But we'll never know what course Elvis's life might have taken had that book never existed. I know what it did to him. It was an awful thing to witness, and to this day it remains one of my most frustrating and painful memories.

At one time or another, various members of the inner circle have been criticized and even blackballed for publishing or discussing their memories of life with Elvis. We have been accused of "cashing in" or exploiting our association with Elvis Presley for monetary gain. But remember, it's our life story as well, and I believe we have a right to tell it, providing it's the truth. I think it's important some reality and perspective gets introduced into the myth that we're all riding some kind of eternal gravy train.

Firstly, we all invested years and years of our lives into serving Elvis's needs. After he passed away, we received no pension, no percentages, no severance pay, and as you know, no provisions were made for anyone outside of the immediate Presley family in his will. Many of the guys were earning well under $100 a week when they started working for Elvis. Instead of cultivating secure positions in companies and corporations with built-in raises, benefits and promotions, we lived by the seat of our pants. Sure, we had a blast, lived like high rollers and received numerous gifts, cash bonuses and other perks. I am not going to ever belittle how well Elvis treated all of us. But the fact is, when it was over...it was *over*.

Although it was obvious he was physically in trouble, none of us planned on Elvis dying in 1977. We thought he would somehow always make it through and go on forever. Even J.D. Sumner, who was many years his senior, said, "I always thought I would die long before Elvis would." So what profession were any of us, now in our forties, qualified to enter after devoting ourselves entirely to one specific individual who was now deceased? Fortunately for me, my friend, concert promoter Jerry Weintraub, offered me a job in the entertainment field. But many of the other guys were not as fortunate. As I said, we received no severance pay, and most of us had no financial cushion to soften the fall. We all had to scramble to pay the bills and keep our families fed.

The way I feel, in the final analysis, despite what you may have heard over the years from the various rumor mills and gossip sites, we all really made a great team. Elvis surrounded himself with good people, and we all tried our best to keep him safe and happy.

I guess now is as good a time as any to say a few words regarding Red, Sonny and the other fellow members of the "Memphis Mafia".

There's no denying we have all said hurtful things and have been openly critical of one another in varying degrees over the last three decades. During our years with Elvis, we were constantly functioning in a very high-tension environment, always burning the candle from both ends. And in order to keep up with Elvis's pace, many of us began abusing pills and medications ourselves. It was like a wild ride in a rocket ship that eventually crash-landed. The highs were very high…but the lows were very low. Living with Elvis Presley was not always easy. Surviving life after Elvis Presley was not easy, either. It's still not easy. Our years with him have affected our individual lives, dispositions and personalities forever, sometimes for the better...but sometimes not.

The plain truth is we were a bunch of young guys, traveling in the fast lane of life with the brightest star the world has ever seen. We lived upside-down lives where night was day and day was night. We took many absurd risks and made many foolish choices. Quite a few of us lost ourselves, and our families, along the way. We shirked responsibilities, hurt loved ones, and made extreme sacrifices to be with Elvis. But we did so willingly. We were there, and we wanted to be there. We paid a heavy price for that lifestyle...and Elvis paid his. More importantly, we all shared a brotherhood and camaraderie with one another, not unlike the fraternities often found within the military, that could never be duplicated or experienced by any other group of men. We all made mistakes, and perhaps we can never relive the feelings for each other we once shared yesterday. But we had what we had, and it was real. And regardless of what it cost or how much it hurt when I lost it, I would never trade the memory of those days for anything in this entire world. Deep in our hearts, despite the dissentions between some of us, I believe we still love as brothers. We will forever share something unique only a handful of people on this whole earth can claim. I had the time of my life, and I sincerely thank all of them, and especially Elvis, for having been a part of it.

ELVIS & TURNING FORTY

Like most maturing men and women, especially back in Elvis's era, turning forty was considered the first major step toward "old age". Phrases like "over the hill" simply came with the territory. In those days, rock n' rollers were pretty much considered expired milk by age thirty. Today, we have performers like Mick Jagger, Steven Tyler and Rod Stewart who, in their late fifties and mid-sixties, are still considered credible "rock stars". But in those days, the image of a man over forty swiveling his hips to "Hound Dog" held certain "undignified" social implications.

Elvis saw turning forty as a major setback. It should have made no significant difference, and it certainly made no difference to his fans...but you try telling that to him! He more or less succumbed to the stigma that you "weren't a kid anymore", regardless of the fact that in many aspects, Elvis still lived life as a carefree teenager.

The fact that Elvis, the symbol of youth and teenage rebellion in the 1950's, had reached the vulnerable age of forty was not lost on the tabloids. Elvis was goaded in the press, and his developing mid-section lent itself to stinging criticism. "People" magazine even did a cover story. And when late-night television icon, Johnny Carson, whom Elvis adored and watched habitually every night, made some "fat and forty"- type jokes, that really pissed him off and elevated his level of insecurity.

Instead of stepping up his exercise regime and combating the aging process by improving his nutrition and overcoming his drug dependency problems, Elvis instead took a quick fix and had a minor face-lift that was so subtle many of us didn't even notice it. But in his head, it made him feel better.

Once Elvis turned forty, he became a bit more sullen and less outgoing. He would spend more and more time in his bedroom, alone, reading incessantly, searching for clues to his life's purpose. He drifted away from karate, his greatest physical stabilizer and the only true symbol of discipline in his lifestyle. Once these activities were missing from his routine, Elvis began to put on extra weight, which added yet another factor to his already difficult struggle to maintain his youth and vitality.

As he got older, Elvis struggled to compete with the younger image of himself he felt his fans expected. He hated the thought of disappointing them. He knocked himself out trying to live up to the image they held of "Elvis Presley". I wish he could have realized his fans would have accepted him however he chose to present himself. I wish he could have convinced himself he didn't need the jumpsuits anymore, that the fans would love to see him in a simple suit, or some other type of stage wear. But that "if it ain't broke, don't fix it" stigma was etched in his mind. He felt if he changed anything, it would alienate his core audience.

I remember him commenting on Bobby Darin during his "protest" period in the late sixties. He was still the talented Bobby Darin, but without his hairpiece, unshaven, wearing jeans and a denim jacket, strumming an acoustic guitar, and singing all unfamiliar material. Elvis expected to see Bobby in his tuxedo, dynamic and swingin', doing "Mack The Knife" and "Beyond The Sea". Seeing this radically different version of Darin made an indelible impression on Elvis. As an audience member, his expectations were not satisfied, and it forever convinced him to stick with his tried-and-true presentation and repertoire.

Elvis wanted to give his audiences what he felt they expected from him. He grew to loathe singing "Teddy Bear", "Don't Be Cruel" and "Hound Dog", but he knew they were his signature tunes and his fans wanted to hear them because it brought back "the fabulous fifties" and the times of their youth. He understood this and made sure these hits were always included in his shows.

ELVIS & "PRESLEY CENTER COURTS"

By 1975, Elvis's personal physician, Dr. George Nichopoulos, or "Dr. Nick" as he was affectionately called, was part of a growing number of racquetball enthusiasts. Aware Elvis needed some form of physical activity to replace his waning interest in martial arts, Dr. Nick suggested he try out the courts at a local health club Nick had membership in. With Dr. Nick's son Dean's help coaching, Elvis quickly took a liking to the sport, and all the guys began to play there after hours several nights a week. When Elvis got into something, he would do it and do it over and over until he got tired of it, and then he would move on to something else.

We began noticing a rising national interest in racquetball, so Dr. Nick, a real estate developer friend of his, Mike McMahon, and I thought it might be a smart idea to invest in a court of our own. It was a fledgling sport that showed a lot of growth potential, and we felt maybe it could be expanded into a profitable franchise venture. So we decided to discuss the idea with Elvis to see if he was interested in backing us as a partner. We had an informal meeting late one night up in Elvis's bedroom at Graceland, and he was in support of the concept. There was one caveat however. "You've got to talk to my daddy about this. You know he handles these type of things for me," he said.

Elvis's father, Vernon, despite his poor education and lack of any business savvy whatsoever, unbelievably was in charge of Elvis's financial matters! Vernon grew up in abject poverty and, despite Elvis's bountiful success, was terrified his son's reckless spending would somehow plunder the family back into a life of penniless struggle. As a result, he loathed to spend any money he didn't absolutely have to, a critical handicap to the thought process of someone in charge of making bold investment decisions. It was actually quite a ludicrous responsibility for Mr. Presley to endeavor. But he was Elvis's father, and we had to respect his wishes. So we had our meeting with them to discuss our concept for "Presley Center Courts". Now, Vernon had a consistent track record concerning all his financial investments for Elvis...they all consistently lost money! Ironically, the one surefire investment offered to Vernon...he declined! Elvis was offered a sweetheart deal that would guarantee him exclusive control of the Wendy's hamburger franchise for the entire state of Nevada, but Vernon turned the opportunity down. I don't have to tell you how wildly successful Wendy's hamburgers is today.

Anyway, the basic racquetball deal structure went like this: Elvis was to lend the name "Presley" and put up some of the start-up money, about a $75,000 initial investment amount if I recall correctly, and become partners with the three of us in a single Memphis location of Presley Center Courts. If that venue proved successful, we could then expand and franchise across the country. This was an excellent idea in theory. Construction work was eventually started on the Memphis court.

To make a long story short, expenses started soaring, and the project cost a lot more than anticipated. After expenses and loan payments were settled, we were consistently "in the red" as they say, and Vernon became very concerned. Then we came to find out that the partner with us was using some of the racquetball court money to finance the remodeling of his home! Dr. Nick and I were blind to the details of day-to-day operations because we were busy and on the road with Elvis all the time. This was Mike's department of responsibility. Trouble was, we weren't around to watch what Mike was doing.

This revelation did not go over well with Elvis, of course, and when Vernon was told about it, he promptly decided to back out of the deal. Vernon was not happy with this whole racquetball business from the get-go, and this was the perfect excuse he sought to cut his losses. A lawsuit was filed against Elvis for breach of contract, but nothing ever happened with it, and it eventually just went away. Unfortunately, the venture became just one more unpleasant, stressful episode during an already tough time in Elvis's life. Looking back, I wish I had never heard the term "racquetball court". It almost put us all in "bankruptcy court".

The last thing Dr. Nick and I wanted was to cause Elvis any additional stress. But hindsight, as they say, is 20/20. That's the nature of business. It's a gamble. The truth is, Elvis was just not cut out to be a business mogul. He was an entertainer and was meant to stick with that 100%.

ELVIS & DR. NICK

Speaking of Dr. Nick, I must speak frankly in his defense. It had pained me over the years to witness the injustice this man has received, and I am finally going to set the record straight. Firstly, Dr. Nick genuinely cared for Elvis Presley. There is no question about that. Any portrayal you might have seen of him in the media is highly exploitative and sensational. Most of the population formed their biased opinions about Dr. Nick based on the 1979 segment of the show "20/20" hosted by Geraldo Rivera called "The Elvis Cover Up". Because Elvis's drug problem was enabled by prescriptions, many written by Dr. Nick, the press demonized Dr. Nick as a maniacal drug pusher who indiscriminately dispensed narcotics to Elvis like candy. The truth is, he cared for Elvis very much and did the best he could to control and supervise his drug usage despite the very tenuous and difficult situation he was up against.

The dynamic of their relationship was very complex and multifaceted. Beginning around 1967, not only was Dr. Nick Elvis's on-call personal physician, he was also a substitute father figure, confessor, buddy, babysitter, pseudo-psychologist, and all around 24-hour support system. Elvis would think nothing of phoning Dr. Nick in the middle of the night, waking him or keeping him up talking and answering questions until daylight. And Nick never denied Elvis his undivided attention. There were plenty of scurrilous doctors surrounding Elvis that existed purely to exploit him, his pocketbook and his celebrity status, but Nick was not one of them. Dr. Nick was one of the few doctors concerned enough to risk inciting Elvis's wrath by refusing to indulge him if he suspected Elvis would abuse whatever medication he was demanding. Dr. Nick was not perfect, but his sincere intent was always to look after Elvis's well being. He realized what Elvis represented to millions of people throughout the world and did everything he could to preserve his life. He made great sacrifices at his own practice in Memphis to look after Elvis personally because he cared so much for him and took this responsibility so very much to heart.

If he, or any of us, fell short of that goal, it was not because we didn't try. It's easy for the general public to judge the situation and criticize our efforts, but they weren't there. The image most people have of Elvis Presley is what they saw in movies and onstage. They were not there behind the scenes, dealing with the day-to-day pressures of his up and down lifestyle. Don't get me wrong; eighty percent of the time I spent with Elvis was an amazing, fun experience. But there were many periods, during the last few years especially, where, frankly, it was pure hell.

The saddest part was that it didn't have to be that way. On numerous occasions, Elvis would clean up his act, lay off the stuff and be the "old Elvis" once again. We would all breath a sigh of relief, look at each other and say, "Hey, maybe it worked

this time." One example I recall is when we went to Hawaii for a vacation in March of 1977. Elvis took the whole gang along with many of their family members, including his new girlfriend, Ginger Alden. The entire time we were there, Elvis was in a great mood. We laughed and played around, and it was just a loose, fun time without any of the perils or concerns of his addictions. He always had to take some type of sleeping medication, because without it, he just couldn't sleep. But overall, he stayed clean for quite awhile, and it proved to us that the heavy medications were just a crutch and that he really didn't need them.

But like any alcoholic or drug-dependent person, once a pressure or bout with depression arises, they reach for that vice they know will numb their problem.

Dr. Nick literally went through hell trying to handle Elvis's myriad of problems. Most people don't realize the extent he went through to help Elvis. And he enlisted many of us to help him. It got to the point where Elvis just wouldn't feel "right" without receiving a daily routine of medications. Many were innocuous, like B-12 vitamin shots or decongestants. But some, like Dilaudid and Placidyl, were heavy narcotics that could yield devastating effects if not strictly monitored. One of the side effects of the substances he was taking were these terrible mood swings. We never knew which Elvis would come out of his bedroom during those later years. And believe me, you didn't want to be around Elvis when he was in a foul mood. Each one of us was on the receiving end of his tantrums at one time or another. We would each silently beg and pray for them to soon pass over. We knew it wasn't Elvis talking; it was the medications. The guy that behaved in this manner was not the guy I met in the Army, not the guy I watched tape the '68 "Singer Presents Elvis" TV special, or the guy I tooled recklessly with around the grounds of Graceland in a speeding golf cart. There were periods that had us all on edge on an almost daily basis. Sometimes he would lash out at us or demand things we knew would do nothing but make his situation worse. We did our best, believe me, but there was a definite limit to what we could forestall. Dr. Nick formed all kinds of plans and schemes to limit his intake or to fool Elvis into thinking he was receiving a medication that was not actually being administered. He also initiated a part time nurse, Tish Henley, who lived in a small trailer with her family on the grounds of Graceland, to dispense carefully formulated packets of medication. That way, Dr. Nick could control and monitor Elvis's exact consumption levels. But even that arrangement wasn't infallible.

Our ongoing predicament was that the fulfillment of any desire Elvis Presley had was only a phone call away. If Dr. Nick refused Elvis something, he would rant and rave, threaten to fire him, or just get it from somewhere else. Elvis would think nothing of getting on a plane and flying to another city where one of his other doctors would eagerly dispense whatever he wanted. Then, once Elvis got what he wanted, all of Dr. Nick's monitored control went out the window. Consequently, if Elvis did a bad show after taking one of these "outside" medications, Dr. Nick's reputation would suffer for it. So Dr. Nick's hands were tied. He was ultimately fighting a losing battle unless Elvis himself agreed to change his patterns. There were too many unscrupulous people willing to aid Elvis with his self-destructive behaviors. Have you any idea what it could be like on a bad day to drag Elvis out of bed, get him alert and awake enough to eat breakfast and help prepare him for his show?

We did everything we could to curtail his intake. The stories you've heard of us emptying pills and replacing their contents with sugar or saline are true. Our resentment over the situation was not because we didn't love Elvis or care enough to inconvenience ourselves. Quite the contrary; it was because we knew, ultimately, that we were inadequately trained to handle the type of medical intervention that needed to take place. We couldn't force him, and no one from the outside was allowed in to help. It had to start with Elvis himself. Whatever was needed of us, regardless of what it was, we all would have done it in a heartbeat to help the man. No question. We all sat for hours, racking our brains trying to devise ways to get through to him or convince him to seek professional help; because as much as it was a physical addiction, it was also a psychological addiction. We all tried independently to reason with him. I did, Sam Thompson did, and Red West had several heated confrontations with him over it. Elvis had convinced himself in his mind that he needed these medications to function.

Like most people who are under the influence of long-term drug abuse, the individual develops a false sense of security and control. Elvis told anyone who tried to reach out to him, "Don't worry about me...I know what I'm doing...I can handle it...I know as much about these medications as my doctor does." Eventually, he grew so weary of facing people, knowing they were aware of his drug usage, that he became more and more insular in order to relieve the burden of his guilty conscience. Elvis always spent a lot of time in his bedroom, but during the later years it was not uncommon for him to stay in there for weeks at a time.

Despite the troubles he was having those last few years, I never expected Elvis to die at age 42. I knew there were some serious close calls and things weren't getting better, but he rebounded so many times before that I figured he would probably outlive us all. He somehow seemed beyond human mortality. When he died so suddenly, I, like the rest of the world, felt robbed. A huge part of my life vanished forever in an instant. I lost my best friend. Once I finally allowed myself to accept that he was gone, my soul felt stripped bare. Elvis's life was not a tragedy; it is one of the greatest success stories of all time. That he eventually succumbed to the pressures of being the great star that he was is the only thing sad I can think of about his life.

Consequently, when Elvis passed away, Dr. Nick was viciously attacked by the media. Elvis Presley was dead, and it had to be blamed on somebody, and his doctor was the obvious choice. He was marked as the scapegoat for every mistake Elvis ever made in his lifetime, as well as taking the blame for all the doctors who *did* harm and addict Elvis to certain drugs. As a result, Dr. Nick was dragged through court, his license to practice was suspended, his professional reputation as a general physician was all but destroyed completely, and he and his family suffered a tremendous amount of undue personal ridicule and abuse. He was even shot at. If any of these people attempting to persecute him actually knew the type of man he was, they would never have done what they did to him. It really is one of the saddest aspects of Elvis's death. If Elvis were here today, I could imagine him saying, "Ladies and gentlemen, this is a good man, and he has done everything to help me." During his trial, I was asked to testify on his behalf, and I did so without hesitation. I knew firsthand that for ten years Dr. George Nichopoulos had run himself ragged trying to help Elvis Presley. And to show you how powerful the media is, even though he was exonerated in three separate trials, the notion still exists to this day that Dr. Nick contributed to Elvis's death. As I said, the public did not know what he was up against as Elvis's doctor. I doubt anyone else in his position could have made any greater progress. Elvis was just too stubborn and too convinced he was in control and knew what was best for him. We have all beaten up on ourselves over the years thinking, "What could I have done differently...and why didn't I do this or that?" It's a very painful situation to contemplate, "Could I have done something extra to save my friend's life?"

ELVIS & THE COLONEL

If there was ever one figure in show business the world will probably never comprehend, it is Colonel Thomas A. Parker, manager of Elvis Presley. He was an enigma, even to me, and I knew him a lot better than most. His unsympathetic, boorish reputation was really a front he used to confound and alienate his rivals or anyone who tried to corral Elvis.

He was a very unorthodox manager, but that suited the picture well because he was managing a very unorthodox career. Again, we must think back to the early 1950's world of show business when the stars of the day were people like Patti Paige, Nat King Cole, Eddie Fisher and Eddie Arnold. The world had never experienced an "Elvis Presley". There was no precedent for a manager to refer to for guidance. Elvis and the Colonel were literally blazing the trail that The Beatles, The Rolling Stones and all the other superstar acts that came much later would follow. By the time The Beatles came to America in 1964, Elvis had already conquered every avenue of show business...almost a decade earlier. There were four Beatles, but there was only one Elvis. That level of hysteria and massive popularity for a performer had never seen before in the music business. It's easy to forget that Elvis and the Colonel were inventing concepts and creating inroads that today are taken for granted.

I can understand why the Colonel has the checkered reputation he does, but I'm certain if Colonel had been a more diplomatic and gregarious personality that catered to the egos and sensibilities of other showbiz big shots, the industry would have painted a much brighter picture of him in the press. But to them, Colonel was an impossible, impenetrable business adversary that took full advantage of every angle and was in utter control of his property, collecting every last possible dollar from their deep, city slicker pockets in the process.

And Colonel was not afraid to play the role of the heavy if it was in his or Elvis's best interests. If he didn't like a deal or didn't want Elvis to do something, he would simply make preposterous excuses or ridiculous demands like, "Elvis will be glad to do a walk-on on your TV show for a small fee...but it will cost you $50,000 for him to walk off," or some such absurdity. And the Colonel thought nothing of blowing off media moguls like Dick Clark, for instance. Consequently, many people in the business grew quite resentful of him and, indirectly, of Elvis. What the big shots couldn't fully control, they tended to dismiss...or destroy.

Elvis needed a buffer like Colonel Parker. Elvis was, by nature, a non-confrontational person. He liked things to be as uncomplicated as possible and didn't care to deal with trivialities or head games, especially where money was concerned. For example, he would pay the full, undiscounted amount for something he was buying rather than bicker and dicker over price. He also hated business. If a stack of papers were placed in front of him to sign, he might ask, "Is everything okay with this?" and then just sign them all without examining a word. In the studio, he'd prefer to get a performance down in one continuous live take, rather that record and re-record his performance to technical perfection. He didn't bother with intricate tax shelters or foreign bank accounts in an attempt to shortchange the IRS. If ever an unpleasantry needed to be handled, it was up to one of us, his father, or the Colonel to resolve. If Elvis preferred to avoid an obligation or decline an invitation, he could disappear behind Parker's foreboding presence. Elvis wanted to have fun, not toil with unpleasant minutiae, and rightfully so. He was the star, and we were there to smooth over the bumps in the road he traveled. I kept track of his expenses, looked after his checkbook, kept track of phone numbers, and initiated most all the communications related to his entire operation. Elvis occasionally made certain personal phone calls on his own, but usually it was, "Joe, get so and so on the phone!" Elvis was a simple guy...he simply wanted it when he wanted it!

Throughout Elvis's career, he was protected and insulated from virtually all levels of personal responsibility. The Colonel would wave his mighty cane, and whatever issue or concern was pressuring Elvis would usually disappear like vapor. You have to understand something; Elvis detested dealing with "stuff", especially business. He just wanted things to be in place and ready to go so he didn't have to worry about anything. The Colonel always saw to it that Elvis was comfortable and his needs looked after. Elvis wanted for nothing. If a problem arose, we were there to tend to it. If it were over our heads, Colonel, his assistant, Tom Diskin, or

Elvis's attorney, Ed Hookstratten, would deal with it and have it taken care of. The Colonel and all of us had our hands full maintaining this type of cocoon-like environment for Elvis, but I have to say we managed to do so for a lot of years with very, very few slippages. If you don't think handling Elvis's career was a 24/7 responsibility, think again.

Perhaps this explains some of the reasons why Elvis never actually "dumped" the Colonel, as so many Monday-morning quarterbacks have suggested. Likewise, where was Parker ever going to find himself another golden goose like Elvis Presley? They were very co-dependant on one another. There were a few times when they had a huge blowout argument, and the process of dissolving their partnership was threatened. At one point during the last year or so, Elvis was considering asking Tom Hulett, Elvis's representative at Concerts West, to manage his affairs. But without fail, the rift between them would invariably settle down, and things would return to their familiar routine without missing a beat. Elvis was simply too comfortable, or complacent, to be bothered making any major changes. Like I said, he was very non-confrontational and would usually defer to complications rather than fight to resolve them. And yes, quite a number of pitfalls in his career were a result of this lack of tenacity.

But the bottom line is Colonel was able to make deals and accomplish feats typical managers wouldn't have the nerve to even consider. His tactics were brilliant, if sometimes crude. Over the years, I have noticed something very telling regarding the Colonel's reputation. Generally speaking, if you personally knew or worked with him, I bet you dollars to donuts you would be protective and defensive of him, having a much higher appreciation and respect of his genius than any outsider would. He truly was an enigma.

Let's face it; the Colonel had balls! The marketing Colonel masterminded, the merchandising he pioneered, and the demand he created for Elvis by limiting his exposure to the public are just a few examples of his shrewd adroitness. He made deals for Elvis that were earthshaking for their time. Every level of show business that Elvis entered, he conquered. He broke all previous records or received the highest ratings in everything he endeavored: records, movies, television, concerts, merchandising -- you name it. The Colonel had his strengths and weaknesses like any other manager, and yes, he made his share of costly mistakes. If the Colonel gambled away some of his fortune, that was his business. The legacy they created together speaks for itself. How can you argue with the fact that, to this day, Elvis Presley remains the greatest star of all time? The Colonel must have been doing something right!

Also to Colonel's credit, he was a man of his word. If Colonel agreed to something or made a promise or a deal, it was as ironclad as a Fort Knox vault. In a business like "show business", notorious for broken promises and unfulfilled commitments, this meant a hell of a lot. One thing I'll say about the Colonel...even if you very weren't fond of him, you had to respect him. You would probably never know it judging from his public persona, but Colonel was also a very sensitive, caring and hospitable man. And although he had the reputation for being a guy who struggled to part with a dollar, I can't tell you the amount of charity donations he made over the years -- probably hundreds of thousands of dollars. You're probably unaware of this because that's the

way he wanted it, but I assure you, he gave a lot of money and helped out a lot of people. In fact, a large portion of Elvis's concert souvenir concession income was donated to charity.

Elvis's face-to-face relationship with the Colonel was almost always behind closed doors. Regardless of how frequently I might have spoken to the Colonel, whatever he and Elvis discussed was strictly between them. They had that understanding, and that's the way it was the entire time they were together. I was more or less the Colonel's liaison as far as Elvis was concerned. We were with him every day. Colonel was usually either at one of his various offices, or if we were on tour, in a city or two ahead of us doing advance work and making sure things were in place when we arrived the next day. Colonel needed to be kept continually informed of our day-to-day maneuvers so he could best manage Elvis's affairs and tend to his specific needs, which varied greatly depending on Elvis's mood that day. Since I was the so-called "foreman" of the operation, Colonel depended on me to advise him of important specifics, not only concerning Elvis, but also for the entire group. Elvis didn't want to be bothered, so it was up to me to coordinate all the arrangements, schedules and travel plans for an entire organization of many people.

Another great mystery is why Elvis never took advantage of the consistent offers he received to perform outside the United States. It is generally believed that the Colonel put the kabosh on these foreign trips for his own selfish purposes. The fact is, Colonel refused to make arrangements to bring Elvis overseas until he cleaned up his act. Elvis could get away with carrying and transporting his drugs and guns across state lines and aboard planes in America, but in foreign territories, Colonel was sure the press and the authorities would catch Elvis with something, and the results would have been devastating embarrassment and scandal. We couldn't take the risk. Elvis never cleaned up his act, so we never played outside of the US; it's that simple.

The Colonel was well aware of Elvis's physical troubles, and I'm sure he discussed helping him with them. But as I said before, you couldn't tell Elvis anything he didn't want to hear. He would say, "Thank you for your concern, I appreciate it, but I'm fine and I know what I'm doing." The Colonel resigned himself early on to stay out of Elvis's personal life. They had their professional roles in their relationship, and never the twain did meet. But let's face it, you don't work with someone for almost twenty years, see they are in trouble and not say a word about it to them. Of course the Colonel was concerned. He always asked me, "How's he doing today?" or, "What can we do to help him?" But the Colonel, like Dr. Nick, could only do so much. If his father was powerless to control his own son, what could we possibly have done? Elvis would let no one interfere with his personal agenda.

Much criticism has been leveled at Colonel for arranging Elvis's last television special, and "allowing" him to be on camera when he was in such obviously poor health. But when the deal for the CBS "Elvis In Concert" television special was first brought to the table, Colonel arranged the production date far enough in advance that there was plenty of time for Elvis to prepare. A considerable offer was made by CBS, and quite frankly, Elvis needed the money. It was his decision to do the special. If he had said, "No", that would have been the end of it right there. The Colonel was absolutely concerned about Elvis's appearance, but we assumed Elvis's pride would not allow himself to stay that way for the special. For the record, the special is not literally a document of his "last concert" as is often claimed. The broadcast special was compiled from two different shows taped during his final concert tour.

The Colonel knew Elvis rose to meet challenges in the past, as he did for the 1973 Aloha satellite special. At that time, he went on a strict diet in late 1972 and lost about 25 pounds, so he was in perfect shape for the taping of the concert in January. So we figured this TV special would represent the new challenge that would spark Elvis's incentive as it had before. Our hope was that Elvis, knowing he would again be facing the unflinching eye of television cameras, would do what he had to do to whip himself back into shape. He made his half-hearted attempts, but by June of 1977, the actual tape dates of the concerts, the news of the West-Hebler book had long since taken its toll. Elvis just didn't care enough to be bothered anymore. By that time his attitude was, "What's the use?" Sadly, within eight weeks he was dead.

During the summer of 1976 as Elvis's health became a growing concern, the Colonel discussed the situation with Vernon and suggested Elvis take a 6-month break from the road to rest up and resolve whatever health issues were troubling him. But Elvis himself insisted "no". In fact, he stepped up his performance schedule in 1977. Outside of performing, there was really not much that enthused him. He was just bored. Aside from the time spent with his daughter, things seemed played out to him. He would rather be onstage in front of his fans, making them happy and receiving the love and adoration he needed to feel from them. It helped energize his spirit and keep his mind off his woes. The Colonel was obligated to book tours if Elvis wanted to perform them. Likewise, Elvis was in turn responsible to fulfill his professional obligations. The Colonel became overtly frustrated whenever Elvis's physical condition would jeopardize doing a good show. The performances had become erratic and varied greatly in quality from show to show. We would all be on eggshells wondering if he were going to make it or if we would have to cancel due to illness. This created tremendously difficult situations businesswise. Elvis was not a child. If he insisted that Colonel continue booking tours, it was his responsibility to be physically sound enough to perform them.

The Colonel was a character, that's for sure. But he was not a mean-spirited person. And like Elvis, he was a one-of-a-kind original. If you were to speak to fifty people who knew him, you would get fifty different accounts of what Colonel was like because he related to each person differently, depending largely on how that individual reacted to him. Not much is known about him personally, or how he came to achieve the incredible showbiz flimflam he possessed. His background in the carnival business no doubt lent itself to his unsinkable sense of promotion, hucksterism and ballyhoo. He would never grant interviews, claiming he was saving his trade secrets and showbiz anecdotes for his autobiography, reportedly titled, *How Much Does It Cost If It's Free?* Unfortunately the Colonel passed away in 1997, leaving us with many more questions than answers. If Colonel had ever written that autobiography, I can tell you for certain that it would have become the best-selling book in the annals of the publishing industry!

So no one person, except perhaps his wife, can give you any definitive portrait of exactly who the Colonel was. As for myself,

I thought he was a hell of a guy, and I know I learned a lot from him. He cared for Elvis, and although they had their moments, I know Elvis cared for Colonel.

The bottom line is, regardless of what is ever said, or not said, the team of Elvis and the Colonel represents the most successful union of star and manager in the history of show business.

ELVIS & HIS MUSIC

Music to Elvis was his life's blood. He lived to sing, and he sang to live. I believe he was destined from birth to be "Elvis Presley". I'll tell you something about Elvis -- he was the most natural talent that I've ever heard or seen. Funnily, he was also one of the most un-technical people I've ever known. Until the day he died, I don't think he possessed even the most rudimentary knowledge of his craft. Everything he did was natural and innate. He wasn't a music student; in fact he did poorly at the subject in school. And he never took a lesson. Yet his "feel", his pitch, his creative edge, his expressiveness, and his power were all on point, and from a very early age. Even at twenty, he possessed the experienced vocal prowess of someone over twice his age. It is almost supernatural how he sang. His entire career seemed guided by the stars. Many people feel he was a gift from God, and I must say I agree.

In the fifties, Elvis dared to be different. He dressed different in school, and he looked different walking down the street. He wore his hair unusually long in the days of flattops and crewcuts. When it came to his career, he stepped out on a limb and broke down the walls of musical segregation. His recording of "That's Alright Mama" is widely considered one of the most significant recordings of the century. It certainly lit the fuse of what exploded into what we now refer to today as "rock n' roll".

If anyone had to describe Elvis's performance style during his early days, it would have to be "raw". And he was "real", 100 percent. And whatever he sang conveyed a sincerity, integrity and excitement that have never been matched. He could drive an audience absolutely wild just by walking onto the stage. There was only one Elvis, and within historical context, there couldn't possibly be another like him. What he did, he did almost single-handedly. In the 50's, with band-mates Scotty Moore, D.J. Fontana, Bill Black and the visionary talents of producer Sam Phillips, Elvis forged a path in music that opened the floodgates for all others to follow in behind. Once Elvis appeared on the scene, music was changed forever. His wide variety of influences attracted a wide variety of listeners. His music did not cater to any one race or religion. It was all-inclusive and universal. The fact that Elvis sang all genres of music, and sang them all equally well, separated him from most performers who were "specialists" of a particular style. Incidentally, one person Elvis always felt did not receive the recognition she deserved for helping his career was Marion Keisker, the secretary at Memphis Recording Service where Elvis made his very first recording. She was actually the first person to ever record his voice. Sam Phillips is usually sighted as the man who "discovered" Elvis. But Elvis was well aware that if it hadn't been for the thoughtful foresight of Marion Keisker, he might never have been heard by Sam Phillips; and the name Elvis Presley could have slipped through the cracks of showbiz history.

There wasn't a day that went by that Elvis didn't involve himself in music in some way. He was either performing it professionally or he was singing for himself, harmonizing with friends, or tapping his foot and singing along with a phonograph or radio. Wherever Elvis was, his music was with him. He knew thousands of songs. He surrounded himself with talent and traveled with his own personal vocal groups and musicians so he could jump into a song and have accompaniment whenever the feeling came over him, which I'll tell you was often. Our close buddy the late Charlie Hodge, who was around Elvis as much if not more often than I was, would play guitar or piano and harmonize with Elvis all the time. He was also his musical "sounding board". Charlie would help Elvis select new material, keep track of the music charts and lyric sheets, and was very involved in helping Elvis pace and format his stage shows.

Elvis's premiere musical interest was gospel, gospel, gospel. To this day, whenever I hear a gospel tune, whether it's Elvis singing or not, I think of him. Gospel music was one of his life's major passions. I would almost say he was fixated on it. He knew virtually every religious hymn and spiritual by heart. He even memorized each song's individual vocal parts. In fact, his secret desire was to be a bass singer! Elvis's very favorite singers are probably names you aren't very familiar with: gospel voices James Blackwood, Hovie Lister, Jake Hess, "Big Chief", and "Cat" Freeman, to name the top five. That's one reason he adored J.D. Sumner so much and involved him as much as possible in all aspects of his music. Elvis was a J.D. Sumner fan since he was 14 years old and looked up to J.D. much the same as many of Elvis's own fans look up to him.

Elvis appreciated all types of music, but his main favorites would have to be gospel, country, and rhythm and blues. Rock n' roll and classical were probably tied for fourth position. The only music he wasn't crazy about was show tunes and jazz, although he did appreciate them and even recorded some songs in those styles.

Around the house, he had a jukebox stocked with all his favorite songs, mainly popular tunes from the era of his pre-teenage years. He had a huge record collection that ran the musical gamut, including spoken word recordings. One of his favorite albums was a spoken word LP recorded by French actor Charles Boyer. He would constantly make lists of records he wanted us to find for him. Sometimes he would send us out to get the entire collection of whatever records were in the top forty that week!

Elvis rarely played his own records. I have heard some of the actresses he worked with say that on the set, he would sing to his records in his dressing room trailer, but that was probably to make an impression on them! Around us, he listened to gospel quartets or popular vocal groups from the 50's like The Platters and The Ink Spots, or singers like Jackie Wilson, for whom he had the utmost respect and admiration. Jackie was probably Elvis's favorite entertainer that we saw perform live. In 1975, after Jackie Wilson suffered a paralyzing stroke that ended his career, Elvis generously contributed to his medical expenses and healthcare.

He loved the voices of Johnny Mathis, Karen Carpenter, Anne Murray, Dean Martin, Roy Orbison, Sam Cooke, Mario Lanza, Billy Eckstine and especially Mahalia Jackson and Roy Hamilton. He was crazy about James Brown, Bobby Darin and Sammy Davis, Jr., as onstage performers as well. He and Tom Jones had a mutual respect for one another that was tinged with a pinch of good-natured rivalry. Glenn Campbell, Vicki Carr, Bill Medley, Don Ho and Nancy and Frank Sinatra were good friends also. Just about any top name act in the business was welcome backstage as long as they were respectful and courteous, which they were. Being a southerner, Elvis also had a special kinship with all the major country performers like Johnny Cash, Jerry Reed (who wrote some marvelous songs that Elvis covered including "Guitar Man" and "A Thing Called Love), Dottie West, Kenny Rogers, and Jimmy Dean, etc. Two Dolly Parton songs Elvis wanted very much to record, "Coat Of Many Colors" and "I Will Always Love You" unfortunately were never cut because Dolly (wisely, I guess) refused to relinquish the required percentage of her songwriter publishing.

Although he was dubbed "the king of rock n' roll" early in his career, a title I always felt limited the scope of his musical appeal and influence, Elvis never really associated much with the "rock n' roll" community. To be honest, he just didn't feel that comfortable in that environment. He, of course, was closer with peers from his era like Fats Domino, Chuck Berry, Jerry Lee Lewis and Pat Boone. He recognized the talent and influence of The Beatles and recorded some of their songs as well. He related to their wild success because, next to himself, they were the one act that rivaled his impact and influence. The famous 1965 meeting between Elvis and The Beatles has been told and retold many times, so I won't go into it again here, but he definitely thought they were responsible for making some very important music.

I know he greeted Led Zeppelin backstage at the LA Forum in 1974, mainly because his stepbrothers were Zeppelin freaks. He wasn't into their music at all, but you would never know it by the way he welcomed them. He was so nice to them and treated them as his peers. Those guys, especially Robert Plant and Jimmy Page, were beside themselves with awe when they met Elvis. He was their idol! Lead guitarist Page told Elvis that he was knocked out by his early Sun records when he was a boy, especially the guitar playing of Scotty Moore, and that those records are what made him decide to pick up a guitar and become a musician. Robert Plant echoed Page's sentiments, sighting Elvis as the reason he became a singer. They left the dressing room that night on a cloud, singing Elvis songs out loud as they trampled down the hallway!

Elvis also met briefly with Eric Clapton, George Harrison, Elton John, Brian Wilson, Keith Allison and the other guys in "Paul Revere and the Raiders". I'm sure there were many others. The truth is, anyone who was anyone in music sighted Elvis as an influence. His music transcended all musical boundaries and color lines.

Regarding his own music, as I said, Elvis rarely spent much time with it once it was finished. There were favorite songs of his he would sing, like "Lawdy Miss Clawdy", "I'll Remember You" and "Spanish Eyes", but he was not a student of his own career. He sang what he liked, what made him feel good. And that was mainly gospel. He would often grab a guitar or sit at the piano during an intimate gathering and accompany himself for an impromptu performance for family or friends. I wish one of us had the foresight to document some of these times with a tape recorder, but

Elvis was just having fun. And to be honest, being around Elvis as much as we were, I guess we just took such moments for granted.

Another funny thing about Elvis and his own records -- Elvis couldn't tell you which song was on what album. He couldn't care less. He took little interest in the song selection, track listing, artwork, the album title, or anything that went into the marketing of his music. He felt his job was to choose the songs and do the best he could at delivering a great performance. In the studio, his focus was on the musicians and creating and choosing the finest possible master take. Once that was determined, Elvis forgot about it and left the rest of the details to his producer, Felton Jarvis, the Colonel and Joan Deary at RCA records.

As far as album covers and packaging, Elvis left that up to the Colonel and RCA as well. After around 1969, he refused to sit for formal photo sessions. He had spent the majority of his career sitting for photographers and posing for Hollywood publicity photos. It was something he never particularly cared for and felt uncomfortable doing. I know that sounds hard to imagine considering how photogenic he was and how much enjoyment he appears to be having in the photos! After the "return to Vegas" era, it was up to the Colonel to obtain photos any way he could without Elvis having to sit for them. That is why most every picture you see of Elvis from 1970 onward is either a personal candid or a photo taken onstage during a performance.

ELVIS & HIS FANS

Aside from his immediate family, Elvis's greatest love of his life was you, his fans. His fans meant more to him than just about anything. He fully realized that without your love and support, he probably would have remained driving a truck or hammering out a meager living in some laborious trade. If I were asked, "Joe, what did Elvis love more than anything?" I would have to say, "his audience."

In all the years I was with Elvis, I rarely ever saw him refuse an autograph or decline a photograph with a fan, and even then only if there were some pressing extenuating circumstance. He knew that without his fans, he would be unable to exist. He relied as much on you to uplift his spirits as you relied on him to uplift yours. During the toughest times of his life, the one solace he knew he could rely on was the love and support of his audience. No matter how poor he was feeling or what troubled his mind, he knew he only had to walk onstage to be healed emotionally by the intense energy of the adoring crowd.

If there was one thing Elvis stressed to all of us time and time again, it was, "Be good to my fans -- they are responsible for where I am." He admonished us to never be curt or disrespectful to any of them, regardless of the circumstances. The security teams that worked with us all had strict instructions to look after the fans' safety and be sure no one was hurt or injured should the crowds get a little overzealous. Every precaution was taken to ensure Elvis had safe but open exposure to the crowds that gathered whenever we were in public. Whether it be entering or leaving a hotel, or wherever, we were instructed to protect Elvis, but to try and allow the fans to have a glimpse of him, take a picture or, on some occasions, shake hands and sign autographs.

I have been involved in show business a long time now, and I have worked with many, many of the great stars. I can say without reservation that Elvis Presley possesses the most intense, loyal and passionate relationship with his audience, which as you know has grown even more massive and worldwide since his passing. His primary goal was to please them. If ever he left the stage feeling he didn't do a great show, he would beat up on himself and get into a funk if he thought he disappointed his fans. Immediately after a performance, having just slammed the doors of our limousine, Elvis's first concerns were about the show: "How did we do", and "Was the sound okay?" If he were unhappy with his performance, he would openly criticize himself or make suggestions to someone like Charlie Hodge or conductor Joe Guercio on how things could be improved in the next show. Once, when he felt the sound system had caused a poor show, Elvis asked us to see if we could arrange to have the entire audience's money refunded!

The pre-Army days of his career are widely regarded as his greatest. It is indisputable that Elvis was an "atomic-powered" performer as a young adult. But I think it would be selling him short to argue that the various transformations of Elvis's post-Army career did not yield as many highlights.

You would think that as he got older and was "not a kid anymore", to use his lingo, the mania that surrounded him would subside. But the opposite was true. As he matured, the fans' appreciation and respect for him grew. His popularity never peaked -- it only seemed to expand and become more monolithic. He may have peaked as far as having hits on the record charts, but his amazing ability to move and enthrall people only grew more intense as time went on. There were nights when Elvis was so "on" that I thought the building might collapse from all the movement, wild applause and sheer emotional thunder created by thousands of people going absolutely crazy!

Sometimes during the last few years, Elvis would obviously not be feeling that well onstage. If the fans sensed he was having a difficult night, or needed their strength, the crowds would rally and get twice as loud and supportive. I remember a tour we did in May of 1977. Elvis was very troubled and was not looking his best. The audiences, however, were so vocal, so animated and so hysterical that it was if it were the summer of 1956! They blindly accepted him.

Believe it or not, though, in a way I wish the fans had been more critical. Elvis was the type of person that would get away with anything he thought he could get away with. If his audience loved and accepted him looking overweight, what was his incentive to keep in shape? Regardless of his appearance, or the quality of his performance, the audience cheered, the women swooned and the shows were sell-outs. An obvious drop off in attendance or negative public reaction would have hit Elvis's ego like a ton of bricks, and it might have forced him into a corner. Get in shape...or else! But as I said, Elvis's fans, if anything, got more manic as the years went on. It was a "Catch 22". Elvis was trapped in a web of so many difficult life circumstances; it's really a wonder he coped with it all as long and as well as he did.

But he adored his fans. He spoke of them all the time -- what they meant to his life or how he wished it were feasible for him to get to know more of them on a personal level. Throughout his career and into the late 1960's, he would spend many hours signing autographs, posing for photos and speaking with fans that waited outside the gates of his various homes in L.A and Memphis. But after the infamous Tate-LaBianca Manson murders in 1969, and the death threats and paternity suits of the early 70's, this became a much rarer occurrence. There were also many, many times when Elvis would come to the rescue of fans who needed help financially. I have seen him pay for operations, plastic surgery, medical care, airline tickets, funeral expenses, and buy cars, cover mortgages and sometimes even arrange employment opportunities. He took a very personal interest in a local Memphis fan named Gary Pepper, a young man who organized one of his earliest fan clubs called "The Tankers". Gary had severe cerebral palsy and could hardly articulate his thoughts verbally. Elvis took Gary into his heart and often visited him at home, gave him many personal items, paid for his healthcare, hired his Dad as a gatekeeper at Graceland, arranged for his travel and visits to Elvis's concerts and even invited him to attend his wedding reception. For over 17 years, until Elvis's death, there were arrangements in place to take care of Gary. There were countless others that he helped. I know because he had me write the checks. I wish I had a list of them all. Elvis knew his life was all about entertaining and making people happy. Ask anyone who had the opportunity to meet Elvis Presley and I'm sure you'll hear an awe-inspiring story, delightfully told and with a broad smile. Let's put it this way, it was not something you were likely to ever forget.

He always took time to make someone feel special. He remembered names of people he hardly knew or had just been introduced to. It was amazing. I don't know where his brain stored all the information, but he had an uncanny memory.

He changed people's lives whether he ever actually met them or not. He knew his music touched people and affected them very personally. Each song he chose to record was thoughtfully considered. He wanted to be sure the sentiment, the message, and the feeling the song would create would have an uplifting effect on the listener. He knew his fans turned to his music in times of trouble, and he wanted his "voice" to be a source of hope and inspiration for them. The song "Bridge Over Troubled Water" comes immediately to mind. That lyric, and also the song "Let Me Be There" describe perfectly the type of spiritual haven Elvis represented to his fans.

It's obvious his love was taken into your hearts. Although he has been gone over thirty years, he remains the top entertainer of all time. His fans are the ones responsible for keeping his legacy, his music and his memory alive. It's you that have made this achievement a reality. And I don't think Elvis would mind if I were to say on his behalf, "Thank you all very much."

ELVIS & PRISCILLA

Looking at a photograph of Elvis and Priscilla together, one might imagine the pair as a finely chiseled masterpiece designed to perfection by some grand, master sculptor. They quite simply made one of the most stunning-looking couples you could ever imagine. Something that always amazed me was that Priscilla very much resembled a female version of Elvis! It is no wonder their only child, Lisa Marie, is their spitting image.

The fabled story of their meeting and courtship has been told many times before. It was a fairytale romance that, although ending in divorce, was a love that lasted until the day he died.

I was privileged to accept his invitation as co-best man with fellow Memphis Mafian Marty Lacker at their wedding in 1967. Elvis, Priscilla, and I were very close and spent a great deal of time together in those days. Needless to say, I have shared a lot of treasured moments in Priscilla's company, and we remain dear friends today.

If I had to choose a happiest moment I ever experienced with Elvis, it would have to be the day he laid eyes on his newborn daughter for the first time. He was on a cloud. And proud! I wish I could have frozen the happiness of that moment in time for him and Priscilla forever. Absolute, total joy is the only way I can describe it.

The trouble was, once Lisa Marie was born, exactly 9 months to the day of their wedding date, Elvis developed a complex soon after where he would avoid intimacy with Priscilla once she bore a child. It is a psychological sexual phobia many men suffer from. As a result, Priscilla's physical needs and expectations as a married woman were doomed from the beginning. He loved and cherished Priscilla from the bottom of his heart, I know that for a fact, but between the time they met (she was only 14 at the time) and the time Lisa Marie was born, they had outgrown the relationship. Priscilla had matured into an adult woman. She was no longer the same naive, lovesick little schoolgirl he met in Germany. There were many aspects of Elvis's behavior that never evolved much past the emotional maturity of a teenager. He always purposely sought young, impressionable girls that were more prone to conform to his unusual lifestyle. However, he hadn't banked on Priscilla's emotional expectations to shift as much as they did once they were man and wife.

Lisa Marie's arrival should have been the moment when Elvis said, "Look, fellas, I'm married and have a baby now. We can't go on running around wild like bachelors anymore." It was reasonable for Priscilla to anticipate, once they settled down and had a child, that Elvis should adjust his freewheeling lifestyle accordingly. But married life never changed Elvis's behavior one iota.

Things were different for a while, but it wasn't long before we reverted to carrying on like a bunch of horny college frat boys. Priscilla never outwardly encouraged him to forfeit his career, but she had every right to expect there to be some major changes in the dynamic of their relationship. She wanted some privacy in her home with her husband, without a group of guys hanging around 24 hours a day. But it never happened. Elvis struggled so much with the idea of his long-term commitment that at one point not long after their wedding, he approached Priscilla and asked for a trial separation! That had to be devastating to her. Nothing came of it, and he never mentioned it again, but Elvis clearly had some deep-rooted insecurity with the institution of marriage that was never fully resolved.

They had some wonderful years together, don't get me wrong, and they were very close for a very long time. They shared a special closeness that was surpassed only by the bond he had with his mother. He cared for Priscilla second only to his own parents. But, Elvis just could not devote himself exclusively to one woman. I often quote the phrase, "We weren't married...our wives were."

His marriage and the birth of his daughter were followed, ironically, by the greatest resurgence in his career since the 50's. In June of 1968, just four months after Lisa Marie's birth, Elvis began blazing a comeback trail that started later that year with the broadcast of his first television special, "Singer Presents Elvis", (commonly known as "The '68 Comeback"). This was followed a year later by his long-awaited return to live performance with a smash, kick-off engagement in Las Vegas that set the trail he would follow the remainder of his career. From 1969 onward,

Elvis was constantly traveling, performing, winding down or gearing back up for more live shows. His life became an endless series of sold-out concert engagements alternating between Las Vegas, Lake Tahoe and cross-country one-nighters. In 1974 alone he performed a staggering 152 concerts. That's almost one every other day!

This constant touring served only to hasten the cracks that already existed in the foundation of their marriage. Eventually, except for opening and closing nights in Vegas, there was a strict "no wives or girlfriends" policy. Priscilla and Lisa Marie ended up spending most of their time at Graceland, keeping company with Elvis's cousin, Patsy, Billy Smith's wife, Jo, Grandma or Elvis's father and his second wife, Dee Stanley. She took dance and ballet classes to fill the void and occupy her time. We had to feel for Priscilla. She waited eight long years for Elvis to settle down with her, and a year after her hopeful dreams finally came true, she was left alone once again, this time with the added responsibility of raising a child.

At the time they were married in May 1967, Elvis was bored out of his mind, and his career had been stagnating for years. Ever since the arrival of The Beatles and the accompanying 1964 "British Invasion" of America, he had been in a creative tailspin, churning out several cookie cutter-type "travelogue" Elvis pictures per year. The majority of his record releases were the songs featured on the film soundtracks. He had ceased being relevant to the contemporary rock scene. His creativity and innovativeness were stifled by the confines of movie studio contract parameters that kept him on the big screen, but off the live stage. He lost complete touch with his audience. He grew to detest doing the films, but was always professional, on time and did exactly what was asked of him. Perhaps it would have served his career better if he were more rebellious about going through with projects that went against his better judgment.

In comparison to the grueling concert tours of the 70's, Elvis's schedule during the movie years was considerably lighter. Principle photography usually lasted six to maybe eight weeks at the most. And it would only take him several days to record the soundtrack numbers. That left a lot of free time, even when making three pictures a year. So during the Hollywood years, 1960-1968, he was still able to spend a significant amount of time in Memphis with Priscilla. But once Elvis hit the concert stage again, it was a completely different story. We were at Graceland perhaps several months total out of the entire year. They simply weren't able to spend much time together anymore, and intimacy had all but left the relationship completely.

Elvis was having the time of his life in 1969, 1970 and 1971. The newness of performing live again had not yet grown stale. He quickly became addicted to the rush of adrenaline he experienced appearing in front of a live audience. He was glad to be back out there again, face to face with his fans, feeling the immediacy and excitement only a live audience can create. He was also rejuvenated creatively, and this period of his career is widely regarded as his greatest era since the 50's. He even started having hit records again, something that hadn't happened in quite a few years. But as this new career focus took hold, with all this constant activity swirling around him, he was more prone to neglect Priscilla than ever before. He was the subject of outrageous adulation from all types of women, and although he was undisputedly a "napalm bomb guaranteed to blow your mind", his ego constantly sought the reassurance and validation only a newfound female admirer could provide. And remember, the country's sexual mores had changed drastically since his last days on the road in the late 50's. We were now living in far more liberal and hedonistic culture…the swingin' 70's!

In 1970, he began a secret romance with "the little girl with the high voice", backup singer Kathy Westmoreland. Kathy replaced soprano Millie Kirkham in August of 1970 during a stint in Las Vegas. Although she wasn't the "sexbomb" type like an Ann Margret or a Juliet Prowse, Kathy was a soft-spoken, petite, attractive and elegant lady who shared many of Elvis's religious interests, and they developed an intimate relationship which eventually reverted to a platonic friendship until the day he died.

It was really the old double standard. I guess Elvis was raised with more than a tinge of male chauvinism. He was extremely possessive of his women and insisted they be monogamous, but it didn't always go both ways. If it ever came down to any of us guys being questioned by the wives or girlfriends about anything suspicious or incriminating, Elvis had a patent rule, "…deny, deny, deny". Whenever Priscilla confronted Elvis, he would vehemently deny her accusations. If she persisted, he'd use manipulation: "Goddamn it, woman, I've got enough people bugging me and giving me hell without my own wife riding me too." His explosive, defensive posturing usually worked…or so he thought. She would end up second-guessing herself, apologize, or think to herself maybe she was being paranoid. Elvis's strategy was to make her feel guilty for asking. It might have appeared on the surface that she was fooled, but Priscilla was not so gullible.

I'd like to make it clear that although Elvis had relationships with a wide variety of different women, that did not necessarily mean they were sexual. Patty Parry, for example, was that type of relationship. She and Elvis were dear, close friends since the early sixties. In fact, we all were fond of Patty. What Shirley MacLaine was to the "Rat Pack", Patty was to the "Memphis Mafia". We spent all kinds of time together, but it was purely platonic. In fact, Elvis's nickname for her was "Little Sister". After Elvis passed away, many of the women he spent time with confessed to me later that Elvis simply wanted someone to talk to and unwind with at the end of the night, and that sex was not part of the equation for them at all. He hated to sleep alone and wanted the company of a woman almost constantly. He might read to them for hours, often from the Bible or one of his favorite spiritual books. I also learned he was prone to confide his innermost feelings and reveal sensitive details about himself that he would never discuss in front of "the guys". He was able to show his vulnerable side to women, I suppose, because he associated their attentiveness to the delicate pampering he received from his mother.

The pressures of warding off Priscilla's constant suspicion, though, eventually lead Elvis to make a suggestion that would blow up in his face and destroy a large piece of his world from which he would never fully recover.

Hawaiian-born karate champ Mike Stone was bodyguard for infamous and eccentric record producer Phil Spector. One night, after a Vegas performance in early 1972, Elvis mingled with Stone backstage. Mike Stone was a very low-key guy, and Elvis actually liked him quite a bit. His humble demeanor would never have caused any of us to distrust his motives, so when Elvis suggested Stone give Priscilla private karate lessons, we all thought nothing of it.

Eventually though, some of the guys were convinced Priscilla and Mike Stone were having an affair. In fact, they were sympathetic enough to her situation with Elvis that, in several instances, they discreetly covered for her. I didn't want to believe it, but the notion didn't surprise me. Elvis had neglected her for years. Something like this was bound to happen eventually. Elvis was so secure in his control over Priscilla that he never suspected she would ever turn to another man. After all, he was "Elvis Presley" and she was his devoted wife. He could do what he needed to reaffirm his libido outside the marriage, but she was there to comfort and support his needs. At least that's how he saw it.

Elvis may have been able to carry on his dalliances behind Priscilla's back, but the reverse was just not her style. As the story goes, during his February 1972 Hilton engagement, between shows, Priscilla broke the news to Elvis about her affair, though she didn't divulge Stone's name. Elvis's immediate knee-jerk reaction was to overpower and reclaim his wife by "taking" her then and there sexually. But it was too late; he'd lost her.

Immediately following their separation, Elvis put on his defensive "I don't give a damn" attitude. Inside he knew he "blew it" and was absolutely crushed, but to save face, he felt he had to keep up appearances in front of us. He was also concerned the fans would disapprove of the separation and that his virility would be questioned by his female admirers. For a time, Elvis tried to maintain the facade that he was tough enough to accept his

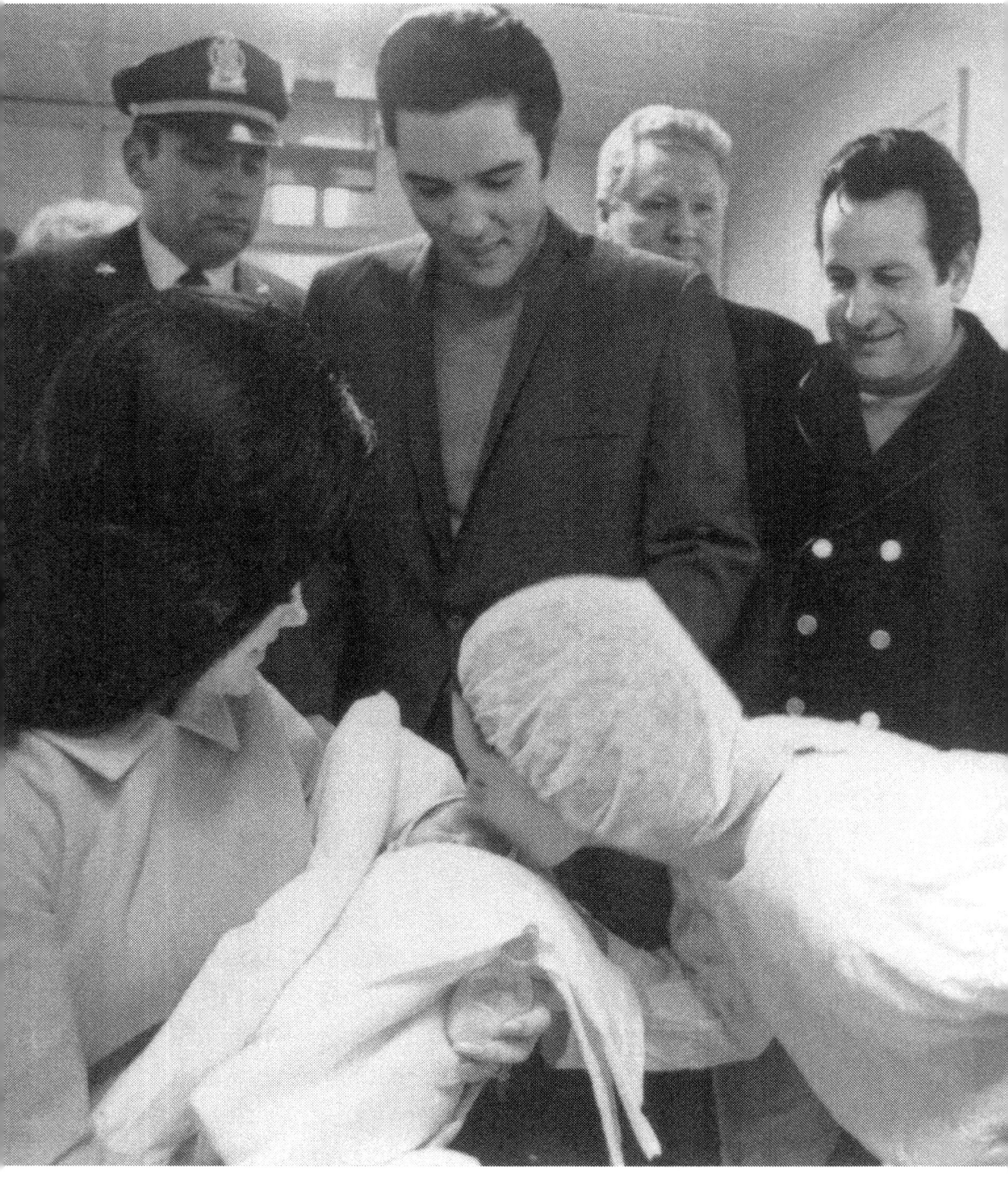

loss and move on, and that he actually preferred his regained freedom. He could never concede defeat to another man, especially one that had claimed his own wife from him. But when he learned it was Mike Store, the very guy he himself had set her up with, he was beside himself with anger. The only outlet for his rage was to vent and threaten Mike Stone through his communications with Priscilla. In a way he was also getting back at Priscilla because he knew his threats were scaring her and disrupting whatever emotional comfort and security she was seeking by being with Stone in the first place.

Finally, when Stone's presence began to interfere with Elvis's visitations with Lisa Marie, he absolutely snapped. That was the final straw. Lisa Marie was his Achilles heel. Anyone or anything that threatened his relationship with his daughter would not be tolerated. At one point, he was also convinced a group of men who invaded the stage and disrupted the show one evening during a Vegas performance were actually thugs dispatched by Stone himself. This notion was later proven to be false, but Elvis was so blinded by rage he was literally stark raving mad. He insisted Red, Sonny and some of the other guys literally seek, stalk and destroy Mike Stone. This sudden outburst occurred in February of 1973 up in his suite in Vegas. He viewed Stone as the embodiment of all his failings, the cause of all his pain. Stone was the man who destroyed his marriage and now threatened his relationship with his own flesh and blood. So during one of his many rages over the situation, he hatched a flight of fantasy plan to have Stone "wacked".

Elvis was livid Priscilla left him, but wasn't he accountable? Didn't Elvis's behavior effectively push Priscilla away from himself and into the arms of another man? Deep inside, he must have realized it was his own fault, but his bruised ego rejected accepting the responsibility. Elvis was not used to suffering the type of indignities experienced by folks living in the "real world".

Eventually, Elvis cooled down. In fact, at one point he wanted to present Stone with a TCB necklace, the symbol worn only by us and select members of the inner circle, as a peace offering. When we heard that, we all went nuts. We threatened to take ours off if Stone received one. It would have diminished its worth and meaning for us. But that was Elvis, always going from one extreme to the other.

Elvis's separation from Priscilla left a void in his heart the size of the Grand Canyon. I hate to admit it, but I'm afraid he was a changed guy after that. The loss of his mother was his first great life-changing experience, and losing Priscilla was the second. Both events altered the course of his life dramatically. Family was a rudder he really needed to help stabilize his life. But it proved beyond realistic for Priscilla, or any woman, to expect Elvis Presley to juggle his career with marriage and fatherhood. In his heart of hearts, it's what he wanted for himself, but his career always took precedence. That realization, coupled with his sexual phobias, made a healthy marriage impossible. Elvis's domestic tranquility was just one more price he had to pay to be "Elvis Presley".

After the challenge and triumph of the "Aloha" satellite show in January of 1973, Elvis's life very gradually began to crack. For the first time in his career he had to cancel engagements due to illness. He was admitted into the hospital in an attempt to detox his system from Demerol dependence and other heavy medications he was abusing through the indulgences of doctors from Vegas and Los Angeles. This was also the first year signs of physical decline were becoming evident to his audiences. His poor diet and prolonged use of tranquilizers only aggravated a congenital intestinal disorder that resulted in a distended colon, creating the appearance of an unsightly paunch. By the time their divorce was finalized in October of 1973, Elvis appeared swollen and bloated, a malady known as Cushingoid, a direct result of cortisone shots he was receiving. This was around the period where Dr. Nick started losing exclusive control of his patient, and as a result, Elvis's health and his performances began to suffer. The year started with one of the crowning highlights of his professional career, but ended with the dissolution of his marriage. He dealt with things the way he usually did when he was depressed...he soothed his hurt with medications and junk food or would throw himself deeper into his work. A few months after their divorce, Elvis embarked upon a full year of constant touring and live performances. The continued on and off again existence on the road increased his need for medications and sleep aids, compounding his drug dependency and reducing time for relaxation and exercise. The habits that increased in the whirlwind performance tours of 1974 manifested themselves into larger problems that had devastating effect on the last two years of his life.

ELVIS & LINDA THOMPSON

In 1972, Elvis was introduced to a Memphis beauty queen named Linda Thompson. Naturally, being a local celebrity, she met and knew a lot of the prominent figures in town. Our buddy, well-known Memphis radio DJ George Klein, was always on the lookout for eligible young females to introduce to Elvis and made the acquaintance of the lovely Miss Tennessee. George really outdid himself with this gal! She was pure as the driven snow and sweet as honey. Linda and her girlfriend, Jeanne LeMay (Miss Rhode Island), were invited to one of Elvis's late-night private movie showings one evening in early July. Later that night at the Memphian theater when the girls were introduced to Elvis, Linda, observing his "costume" of black pants, boots and flowing velvet cape with satin lining, boldly commented, "My, we're dressed like Dracula tonight, aren't we?" Elvis was amused but taken aback. It was an uncommon remark, especially coming from the lips of a soft-spoken southern girl. Most women stammered when they first met him, but Linda was playful and confident, and it piqued his curiosity.

During our all-night movie marathons, Elvis always sat in the front row and always in the exact same seat. When I say "front row", I don't mean Elvis literally sat in the first row of theater seats. I mean the row Elvis chose to sit in (usually about the thirteenth row, dead center) became the "front row", with all friends and guests occupying the rows behind his. It was just one of his little quirks. Elvis constantly made jokes and yelled out one-liners at the actors on the screen. It was funny as hell, really. He often upstaged their dialogue with his hilarious comments. But sitting and actually "watching" a movie with Elvis could also be a very frustrating experience. You might be wrapped up in the plot and enjoying the picture, but if Elvis grew bored or disliked a movie, which he often did, he might suddenly raise his long police flashlight and signal the projectionist, and the film would be abruptly yanked from the screen! Other times, if he favored a movie, or even a particular scene, he would have it rerun over and over ad nauseum. It's a great film, but I doubt I can sit through another viewing of "Dr. Strangelove", one of his all-time favorite Peter Sellers films, for this very reason. Anyway, during this evening in July when he first met Linda, eventually he turned around and noticed George Klein and Linda sitting together. Once he realized George knew her, he excused himself and dragged "G.K" outside to grill him about his alluring new discovery. When he returned, he took George's place in the seat next to Linda, and the small talk began.

When it came time for Elvis to make his play, Linda was standoffish. Her strict moral code would never permit consorting with a married man. But Elvis passionately assured her he was now separated and a "free man", and once the ice was broken, they became quite smitten with one another. But Linda was no hustler. She wasn't some fast moving showgirl-type. A southerner herself, she was raised with many of the same religious values and moral traditions Elvis was. This intrigued him even further because Linda was a challenge. Not only was she stunningly attractive, she was obviously educated and had a marvelous sense of humor. He didn't know it at the time, of course, but she was also a virgin, another definite trait he sought in any woman he might decide to become "serious" with. Elvis knew Linda was a special and coveted personality, and she made quite an impression on him. She made him work a little bit for her telephone number but agreed to visit the house the next evening, which she did with her friend, Jeanne. She was at Graceland until 3 am, and it looked as though they definitely connected in a big way! And then...she promptly disappeared for several weeks! Unbeknownst to us, she went away on an extended vacation with family. Elvis wanted desperately to see her again and had me going crazy calling and calling, trying to track her down. Elvis was impatient, and when he wanted something, he could be pretty obsessive until he got it. By the time she finally returned home, Elvis was already in California preparing to start another Vegas engagement and insisted she join him there. I had her flown in, and before you knew it, they were inseparable. Her presence helped lift the deep sadness he had been wallowing in for months following his separation from Priscilla. "The Lord sent this girl to me," he said. Linda was the person Elvis made the most serious attempt at monogamy with. And I believe they were, at least for their first year or so.

Of all the women that revolved in and out of in Elvis's life after Priscilla, Linda rated highest with everyone. She was nearly impossible to find fault with. Her disposition was consistently upbeat. She was sweet and nurturing, yet she could also hang out and be "one of the guys". She served many different roles in

Elvis's life and tended to all his needs with affection and dedication. She could enter a room and turn heads looking every inch a runway model, or feel just as natural playing the role of motherly caregiver and nursemaid. Linda embodied every supportive, feminine trait Elvis's fickle whims could demand...and then some. By late 1973 she also grew to come to terms with, and reluctantly accept, his perpetual need for the company of other females. Two of the more substantial relationships he became involved in during this era were with Sheila Ryan and Mindi Miller.

It may sound crazy, but that's what living with Elvis Presley could command from people. All of us, everyone around him, would surrender a sizeable piece of themselves for the extraordinary experiences just knowing him and being around him would compensate. It was a severe personal trade-off, yet I can't recall many instances where someone declined a request or an invitation made by Elvis Presley.

Linda had an older brother, Sam, who worked for the Memphis police department. Elvis liked Sam a lot. He was a tall, affable guy who was tremendously capable and responsible in his duties, and Elvis invited him to become a member of the security detail on some of the tours. Eventually, he "stole" him away from the police department, and Sam Thompson became a full-time employee and, along with Dick Grob, another former policeman, worked security for us right until the end. Elvis cared very much for Linda, and he adored the entire Thompson family. He showed his appreciation by purchasing individual homes for Linda, Sam and their parents, and Elvis showered Linda with every amenity and indulgence a girl could ask for. I think if there were a world's record for clothes shopping, Linda Thompson would win the title!

But living day-to-day with Elvis Presley during these increasingly difficult years became very taxing emotionally. Linda was a young girl with her whole life ahead of her. She had personal career aspirations she was willing to put on hold with the hope she and Elvis would start a family. She rode the wave of his up and down roller coaster lifestyle valiantly. It took selfless dedication for a perfectly healthy young girl to lie for weeks in a hospital bed alongside her boyfriend, as she did in 1975 during another of Elvis's hospitalizations. Bit by bit Linda's role in his life drifted from lover to friend to "custodian". On numerous occasions she quite literally saved him from drug-related episodes that might have cost him his life had she not been there to rescue him. More than a few people share the opinion that if Linda had been with Elvis, he might have survived the events of August 16, 1977.

By mid-1976, their relationship was reduced to little more than friendly formality. She drifted into a relationship with David Briggs, an accomplished Nashville session musician who'd replaced Glenn Hardin as Elvis's keyboard player on tour. By this time, Elvis was openly dating other women, even in Linda's presence, and Linda had come to realize there simply would be no long-term future with Elvis Presley. Elvis once said to her, "I'll probably only admit this once, but I have a very self-destructive side."

She was tired of the infidelity, the "vampire" night-for-day existence and the punishing side effects of the pills and medications, the part of his lifestyle she never, ever, accepted or felt comfortable being around. She and others around her were shocked at how much Elvis had changed in just a few short years. He just wasn't the same person anymore. She truly loved him, and I'm

sure has never stopped, but it was tormenting to watch helplessly while someone she cared so much for was self-destructing.

Toward the end of November 1976 Elvis was introduced to a young Memphis girl named Ginger Alden. All his undivided attention switched immediately to her, against his better judgement if you ask me. The most impressive thing I remember him saying about her was that her eyes reminded him of his mother's. Elvis was not thinking clearly. If he was, he would have realized the mistakes he was making.

The handwriting was on the wall. Linda knew she couldn't alter or control Elvis's behavior, and she didn't want to be there to witness the end. Linda had invested almost four and a half years of her life into what was becoming a hopeless fantasy, and for the sake of her own sanity and well-being, she had to move on. She wrote Elvis an impassioned letter, explaining her feelings and concerns, and had it hand-delivered to the house. I knew he cried when he read it, but I'm not certain if Elvis responded to the letter. I don't think he did. Considering the closeness they shared, it was a sadly anticlimactic separation that he barely acknowledged.

Even though he was now separated from Linda, Elvis thought so highly of her brother, Sam Thompson, that he invited him to stay on. With Red and Sonny gone (they were let go earlier that summer), his words to Sam were, "I need ya." Sam elected to stay.

Although it ended with a series of high-watermark concerts that last week in December 1976 had been a very tough year. Elvis's drug dependency was becoming unmanageable, his father was having health problems of his own, he lost two of his closest inner-circle members, he was facing the publication of a potentially lethal expose', and he lost Linda Thompson, one of his main life-support systems. In hindsight, I can see it for what it truly was...the setting for the final curtain.

THE DAY THE MUSIC DIED

On August 15, 1977, I flew into Memphis from Los Angeles. We were scheduled to leave the following day for Portland, Maine, to start another tour. I was staying at the Howard Johnson's motel around the corner from Graceland. When I got to the house around 10pm, Sam Thompson was on duty, and he updated me on the state of events at the house. Sam told me Lisa Marie was still there, that Elvis had requested she extend her visit, and that he would be returning her to Priscilla on the west coast the following day. I wanted to go over some details with Elvis, so I called up to his bedroom. Elvis's cousin, Billy Smith, answered and asked me if it could wait until they returned from where they were going.

Sam informed me that Elvis had a dental appointment, so I waited and chatted with Sam until they came back. When they did, Elvis made a beeline from the front entrance and went straight up to his room. I called him from the kitchen intercom. We chatted for a minute, and I asked him if he needed anything special. "No", he said, "Everything's fine. Just make sure I'm up by four

tomorrow." I didn't realize it at the time, but I had just ended my last conversation with Elvis Presley. I ate a meal the maids fixed for me and returned to the Howard Johnson's to get some sleep.

I arrived back at the house early the following afternoon, asking if anyone had heard from Elvis. They hadn't. The maids made me breakfast, and I settled in the den to make some phone calls regarding the tour.

An hour or so later, the kitchen intercom rang. It was Ginger Alden calling from upstairs. She asked one of the maids to send somebody up right away. Al Strada, one of Elvis's aides, took the phone, listened for a second, and then ran upstairs. Nothing unusual, I thought. Elvis was always calling down for something.

A moment later, Strada called back down. This time I answered. "Joe, come upstairs, I need your help!" he said. His voice was panic-stricken.

I darted up the stairs and into the bathroom to find Al and Ginger huddled over Elvis's obviously lifeless body. The scene hit me like a ton of bricks. Elvis was on the floor in a fetal position, his face half buried in the red shag carpet. The half of him I could see was bluish and contorted. His pajama bottoms were below his knees, his teeth clamped shut over a bulging, discolored tongue. His cherished Star of David necklace dangled below his throat.

I had seen Elvis deathly ill before, but something within me said, "We've lost him this time."

I picked up the phone and summoned an ambulance and then Dr. Nick and Elvis's father. My mind was racing. What should I do? I knelt at the body making futile attempts at opening his mouth, pounding his chest, shocking his system. I was just imitating things I'd seen done on TV in a desperate attempt to get some type of vital sign.

The next thing I knew, people were crowding the bathroom -- Charlie Hodge, Vernon, his girlfriend, Sandi Miller, perhaps others. Emotional chaos was breaking out all around me. Everyone was wailing, crying, praying. I was wide-awake, living a scene straight out of my worst nightmare. Vernon collapsed in a heap. Was he having another heart attack? Little Lisa Marie entered the room just as the paramedics arrived. I shouted to Ginger to remove her as we lifted Elvis's body onto the stretcher and struggled down the stairs and outside to the waiting ambulance. Just as we got there, Dr. Nick screeched into the driveway. Charlie and I jumped in the back of the ambulance with Dr. Nick and sped toward Baptist Memorial Hospital.

Dr. Nick worked desperately on Elvis until we arrived at Baptist. The emergency room doors burst open, and they rushed him to the medical crew known as the Harvey Team, which took over resuscitation attempts. The hospital staff assisted Charlie and me into a private room to wait.

Billy Smith, Al Strada and David Stanley eventually arrived, and we waited for the news together. It would take a dozen miracles to alter the devastating reality we were all bracing ourselves for. As I sat there, numb, replaying what had just happened over in my mind, I realized they were trying to revive a corpse. Who was

I kidding? I knew my best friend was dead the moment I touched him. About twenty minutes later, Dr. Nick entered the room. His face was careworn, and tears streamed from his eyes. "He's gone."

That was it. We all lost it. I felt as if I was having an out of body experience. Half of whoever I was seemed to have just floated off. The remaining part of me shirked the grief and despair of the moment and focused on "taking care of business". I had to remain stoic, at least for now, in order to tend to the mountainous onslaught of media and human panic I knew the announcement of his Elvis's death would unleash. As we suspected, the moment news of Elvis's hospital admission hit the airwaves, the media began to converge. One of my first contacts resulted in a media clip of myself with Charlie Hodge that was filmed at Baptist Memorial Hospital that fateful afternoon. I told the television reporter interviewing me that I had found Elvis's body in his bedroom as opposed to on the bathroom floor. When the reporter then asked me, "Was he lying on the bed?" I said, "Yeah." I have been criticized quite a bit over the years for telling this little fib. The answer is very simple. I stated "bedroom" instead of "bathroom" because I was simply trying to protect Elvis's privacy. Was it really necessary to reveal such an indiscreet, incidental detail like that at such a tragic moment? And remember, this interview occurred within hours of finding my dearest friend dead, the most shocking experience of my life. It was always our job to protect Elvis, regardless of the circumstances. Any answer I gave at the time, especially that soon after, would have been in denial of anything controversial or inappropriate. We were all in a daze, and it amazes me I was able to utter anything intelligible at all that afternoon. For a long time, I functioned on automatic pilot.

My heart and mind were rejecting, as many of us were, the acceptance that Elvis was gone from our lives forever. It took many of us years before we returned to something that even resembled a normal life.

Dr. Nick returned to Graceland to inform Vernon of his son's death. We were terrified the news might bring on another sudden heart attack...or worse. I knew I had important phone calls to make. Charlie and I were brought to an empty conference room where the first number I dialed was Colonel Parker's. Then I called Priscilla, promoter Jerry Weintraub, my girlfriend Shirley, and Sheila Ryan (Caan). Ironically, Sheila was on page number forty-two (Elvis's age) of Red and Sonny's book, *Elvis, What Happened?* when she answered the telephone.

Linda Thompson was notified by Lisa Marie, who phoned Linda all by herself from Graceland. The moment Linda hung up the receiver, every light in her apartment went off. Strangely, in the entire building, only the lights in Linda Thompson's apartment went dark.

Another similarly bizarre thing happened a few days later during Elvis's funeral. Elvis told us once that when he passed away he would find a way to send us a sign from the "other side". As we were carrying Elvis's coffin along the grounds of Graceland, a huge tree limb inexplicably came crashing down right near us. The heavy summer air was stagnant, and there was absolutely no wind or turbulence of any kind which could have caused it to fall. Call us crazy, but we all saw it as some kind of cosmic prank. Each of us later broke off a piece of the limb as a keepsake, so convinced were we that the falling limb was "a sign"... a knowing wink from Elvis!

Elvis Aaron Presley passed away on August 16,1977. I know because I was there when it happened. I ordered the copper casket he was buried in. The man passed away, and it outrages me that so many insidious bloodsuckers have gotten away with trading on the unresolved grief many fans shared over his death. They have invented ghastly stories of family incest, suicide and the faking of his own demise. Every eyewitness sighting, book or tabloid story proclaiming his existence since that date in 1977 have all been perverse, despicable bullshit. Elvis's death impacted the lives of so many millions of people throughout the world, and it has been difficult for many of them to come to terms with the loss. Their emotions did not deserve to be exploited. The worldwide hysteria his death caused continued for many, many years. Perhaps it's easier now to realize how intense the pressures upon him must have been during his lifetime. Elvis "lives"...in the hearts and thoughts of his millions and millions of fans...and most importantly, through the gift of his music. In that regard, yes, Elvis is eternal.

ELVIS & THE IMAGE

Elvis said something illuminating about himself during his June 1972 press conference in New York: "The image is one thing, and the human being is another."

Elvis's fame and success were larger than life. So it was only fitting that his guise onstage was that of a rock n' roll superhero. He was perceived by many as a kind of performing Superman -- an invincible man of power, prestige and indefatigable morals. If you look at the old comic books of Captain Marvel, you will see a character remarkably similar to Elvis's concert persona: spangled jumpsuit, large decorative belt, flowing cape, slick black hair modeled into a tight pompadour. It's an amazing resemblance!

That's because he based his stage persona on such a character. As Elvis revealed during his 1971 Jaycees' acceptance speech, "When I was a child...I was a dreamer. I read comic books and I was the hero of the comic book." Elvis was making direct reference to Captain Marvel! As a child, he viewed the world from the disadvantaged point of a poor southern boy and dreamt of being successful, not so much for himself, but for his parents. He hoped he would someday be able to provide luxuries for them and share his wealth with others. When his dreams came true, that's precisely what he did with his success.

Captain Marvel was the childhood fantasy figure he identified with and ultimately became. Once Elvis was famous, he honed an image that was designed to show his fans, many of whom were very working class, that their dreams were achievable as well. He was a living, breathing representation of their desires and ambitions. He was conveying the message, "Look, see all this wealth I now possess...I grew up poor...you can make your dreams come true also...if you work hard and have faith." He felt his fans expected this type of opulent lifestyle from him. He believed it inspired them to achieve what he had achieved for himself. He obtained a lofty position in show business, but as he also said in June of 1972, "It's very hard to live up to an image, I'll put it that way."

I witnessed first-hand the pressures he experienced being "Elvis Presley", pressures that would have completely crushed a lesser man much sooner than they began to affect Elvis. He never forgot his humble beginnings. He respected and treated all people well. If he showed any favoritism, it was for the underprivileged and needy.

Even as a dirt-poor kid with nothing, Elvis displayed remarkable generosity. Linda Thompson once told me, even as a boy, he would take his comic books and go outside and hand them out to the other poor kids in the neighborhood. I also remember a story where Elvis overheard his dad, who had been out of work, alone, crying to himself that he didn't have enough money to provide for his family. Elvis said a prayer that he would have enough money so he could afford to take care of his mom and dad. Obviously, his prayers were answered.

Touring through Graceland museum today, it would appear that Elvis was a very materialistic person. In actuality, he placed little value on material things. He enjoyed these possessions and used them to entertain his friends and family, but he would just as soon give any of it away…just as he had those comic books as a child. I've seen him do it dozens of times. On several occasions he even handed off valuable gifts to lucky fans right from the concert stage. "They bought it for me, it belongs to them," he would say. He wanted people to have a taste of what it was like to own something they could only dream of affording. It reminded him of when he was a boy, sitting on the corner outside the projects where he lived, watching cars go by. He would pick out a favorite vehicle and say, "I'm gonna own one of those someday." Elvis never forgot where he came from. His humble beginnings and the strict moral code infused in him by his mother were two important stabilizers that enabled him to cope with the temptations and trappings of fame successfully for as long as he did.

Elvis's image was very much a paradox. He felt his talent was a gift from God. He felt a deep responsibility to share and protect the honor of this gift for fear it would be taken away from him should he take it for granted. He was a devoutly religious man, yet he was incapable of being faithful to any woman for any substantial length of time. He read the Bible voraciously and could quote large passages from it verbatim, yet he fell victim to the

insidious trappings of drug abuse. It was a lifelong struggle for him to honor his religious beliefs to the letter, failings you may consider as hypocritical, but at his core he was a spiritual man who passionately believed in God. He pursued his faith in earnest, and if he faltered, prayed for forgiveness. I doubt any one of us could have done substantially better avoiding the pitfalls of success had we been bestowed with his level of power and influence.

I want you to know that at his core, Elvis was a wonderful, decent person. He cared deeply about his fans and sacrificed a great portion of his personal life to please them. He loved his country and supported its military. He was a praying man and he respected people. He honored his parents, cared for his daughter and cherished his friends. He strove to be the pillar of strength we could all rely upon. He rarely complained of his own problems but was always there to listen and help us with ours. His generosity knew no bounds. He lived to make people happy, and he himself was happiest when he brought joy to someone else. I wish there was a way all the good he has done with his gifts throughout the world could be measured. The comfort and enjoyment his music still brings to millions every day is impossible to comprehend. His influence as a performer and as a humanitarian has touched untold millions of people. We can never compile exact statistics, but I believe Elvis Presley will forever remain one of the most inspirational and influential men the world will ever know.

But Elvis was a man, not a God. If some of the things I have mentioned in this book challenge any idealistic portrait some may have of who Elvis Presley is to them, you must realize he was a human being. A very special human being…but he was still only human. He had flaws and failings as every single one of us does. I don't think it's fair that some of his personal shortcomings should in any way taint the incredible reputation he maintained throughout his career as an incredibly giving and caring person. The world today is a lot better off because we had Elvis Presley.

It's important to remember in the world of today, where many top celebrities routinely offend and corrupt their impressionable audiences, that although Elvis had his demons, he never portrayed that side of his nature to his public. Onstage, he made it clear he was there to entertain and make his audience happy. "If we do that, then we've done our job," he would say. He did not abuse the spotlight to further his political agenda, nor did he preach or lecture his audience for or against any belief system or cause. He was aware of his tremendous influence, particularly on young people, and was always careful to be a positive role model for his fans. After he passed, many people just refused to believe that Elvis was imperfect. It harks back to his statement, "It's very hard to live up to an image." Elvis straddled the fence between coping with the pressures of his career and maintaining his clean-cut, wholesome image. He desperately tried to accomplish both for two full decades, and it simply began to wear him out. Elvis did not lead a normal life. He led the life he chose, 100%, but it surely was not normal.

Elvis was not a writer, nor did he do many interviews during his post-Army years. He communicated instead through his music and live performances. One song he recorded in 1971 perfectly conveys his philosophy for those who may have tried to second-guess the perception he had of his own lifestyle. I'm sure that's why he chose to record "Love Me, Love The Life I Lead." It was as if

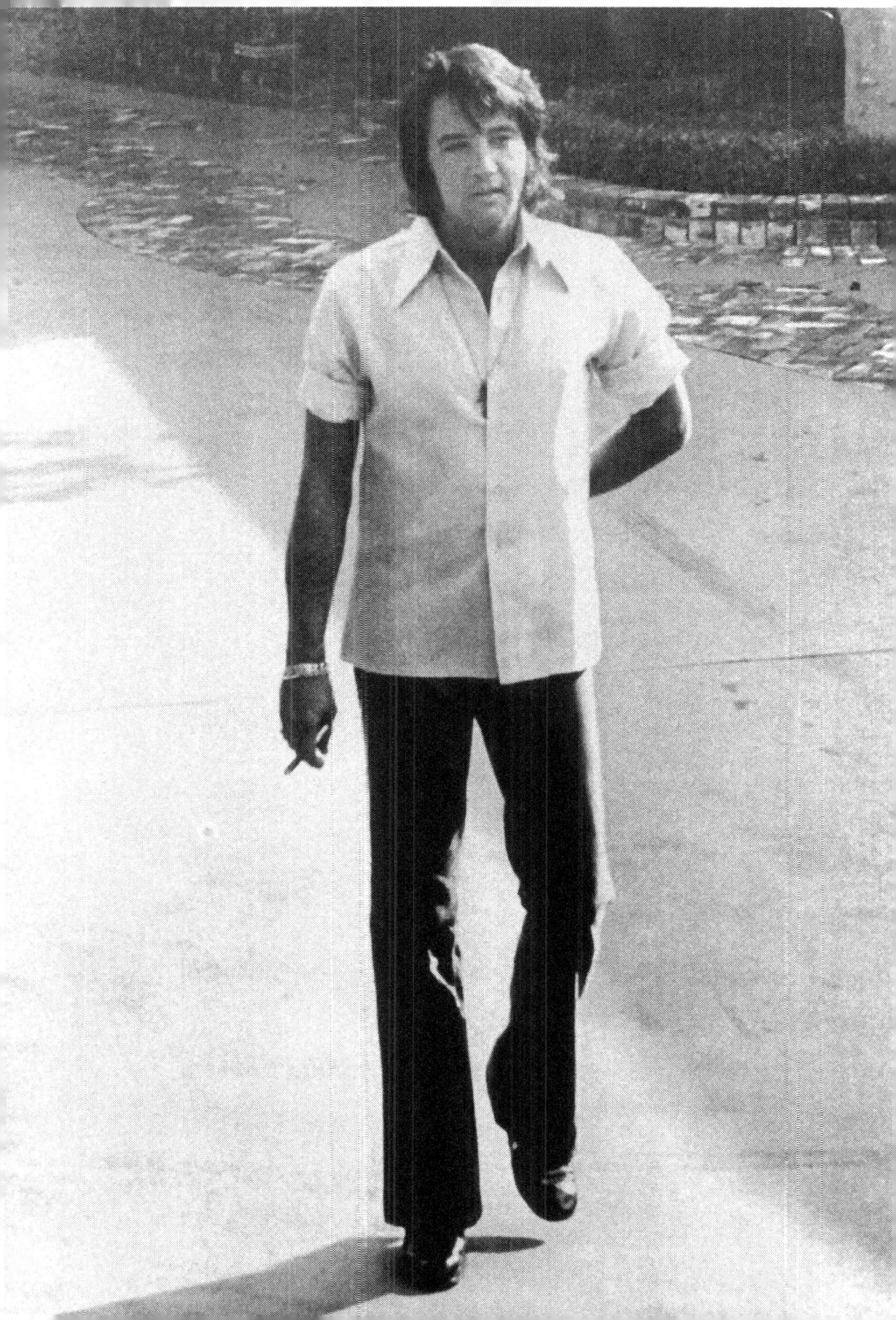

he were using the song to say to those around him, "Look, I was destined to be this guy "Elvis Presley". If you want to be with me, you have to accept me and my abnormal lifestyle at face value. Don't question my needs or my actions. I have to have things this way in order to continue to be who I need to be to the world."

If you're gonna love me, love the life I lead

I need the things I need, don't try to change me

If you're gonna take me, take me for what I am

I can't be another man

I can't be free of the life I lead

By Tony McAulay & Roger Greenaway/PolyGram Int., ASCAP

ELVIS & RECORDING & GINGER ALDEN

When all is said and done, the most important element of Elvis Presley's career legacy is his music. Music is why we know him, what made him a star and what will remain most important in the decades to come. Proof of this is the amazing fact that, three decades after his death, his music is still capable of topping the charts!

Elvis was not a studied vocal technician by any means. He sang with his own natural instincts. He had an innate ability to hone in on the sentiment or attitude of a song, inhabit it with his special magic, and make it his own. He could sing any style of music: rock, bluegrass, country, rhythm and blues, opera, ballads...all with aplomb. Elvis said, "I may not be the best singer in the world, but give me a song and I'll sing the hell out of the son-of-a-bitch." Music was Elvis's life. It was the essence of his spirit. Whatever he sang resonated from deep within his soul. His delivery and expressiveness were uniquely his own and captivated and connected with the listener emotionally. And Elvis's greatest recordings display proof positive what amazing potential he had as an actor. He visualized his songs as living and breathing performances and "acted" the emotions of the song through his vocal delivery.

Elvis was not a songwriter per se, but he creatively refined and personalized the material he performed to perfectly suit his own performance sensibilities. In the studio, he was basically his own producer. There might be a Steve Sholes (1956-1962) or a Felton Jarvis (1966-1977) present to supervise the engineers, keep time and make sure all the technical aspects of coordinating the musicians were in sync, but Elvis selected the master takes, he chose the material he would record and contributed many arrangement ideas as well. Much of the production creativity emanated from Elvis himself, based on his instincts to know what was right. He had an amazing ability to capture the essence of a song's meaning and subtext and how to accent the rhythm of the song with his voice.

Most of the songs Elvis recorded were submitted to him through Freddie Bienstock. Bienstock was Elvis's liaison at Hill And Range, the publishing company that controlled the copyrights to the ongoing roster of songs commissioned for Elvis's consideration. Bienstock solicited the material from various songwriters who were all keenly aware what an Elvis Presley version of their song property would mean in dollars and cents. In return, Colonel Parker saw to it that he and Elvis's publishing companies received a marked share of the mechanical royalties on anything he recorded. As a result, Elvis and the Colonel owned a piece of every song, although neither of them ever actually sat down and wrote one himself. The songwriters' incentive to relinquish an above-average percentage of their tune was the pride and recognition of having it recorded by one of the greatest-selling artists in the history of the business, a fair trade-off considering these songwriters are still cashing handsome royalty checks for their songs until this day. Occasionally, Elvis opted to record outside songs not controlled by Hill And Range -- classics like "Guitar Man" and "Suspicious Minds", for example.

The songs chosen for Elvis's review came to him on specially pressed records called acetates, also known as "demos". Demos are simply produced recordings featuring several instruments and a lead vocal designed to demonstrate the intended feel and style of the song. Many times, the singers hired for these demos would emulate Elvis's voice or vocal style so the song would sound as close as possible to what Elvis's version might sound like.

Elvis's approach to making a record was very unorthodox and quite frankly, somewhat inefficient. The producer, engineers, musicians, background vocalists and other studio personnel would be all set up and waiting, sometimes for hours, before Elvis would arrive. Every one of these people was a union member and was being paid union scale wages. In the studio, time is money. With the number of personnel involved, every hour that ticks by costs a small fortune. Elvis would often arrive late, not because he was being unprofessional, but because he realized the longer the sessions ran, the more money the union members could earn to support their families. In the early days, it was standard business for an artist to cut four sides per every three-hour session. Not with Elvis. If a session was scheduled for 8 pm, it might be midnight before any actual recording took place. When Elvis finally arrived, he rarely went right to work. A specific comfort level had to be achieved in the studio before he was relaxed enough to

start recording. He hated being rushed and would not start until he was ready and the atmosphere was right. It had to be a loose, party-type atmosphere or Elvis just wouldn't get into it. This protocol was actually very effective because the inspiration and joy created in the studio comes across on the records. Elvis's charismatic vibe, meshing spontaneously with the musicians, is infused "live" right into the recording.

Elvis enjoyed recording late in the evening, sometimes throughout the night and into the next morning! He got a kick out of making the record company executives sweat! This worked fine for everyone except Felton Jarvis. Poor Felton, always on a tight schedule, was responsible to the record company for X number of finished Elvis Presley masters being delivered...and on time! So even the slightest delays caused him white-knuckle panic. He was constantly focused on the ticking clock, mentally willing Elvis not to stray from his work. Sometimes Elvis would be on a roll and nail five or even six masters in one session. Other times, it might take a day or even two to finish just one or two songs. It depended on his mood.

Elvis would usually begin a session by going around to each and every person in the studio, from the top musicians to the guy who sweeps the floor, and greet them all personally. Once that was done, he would often sit and chat with the band for a while to loosen up and get reacquainted. Many times he would "warm up" by singing gospel songs, usually at the piano and joined by members of whatever vocal group was working the session. Finally, he would begin listening to the numerous demo records to choose which songs he would like to begin work on. Often, Elvis and the musicians would be hearing the song for the very first time right there in the studio. Sometimes Felton Jarvis knew ahead of time which songs were slated to be recorded and would arrange to have the band start working on them in advance.

I'll give you a general overview of how the average recording session went. Instinctively, Elvis would know if a song was right for him or not. As the songs were auditioned, the discs would be placed into two piles, "yes" or "no". If he particularly disliked a song, he might remove the record from the phonograph and fling the offensive disc across the room! If he heard something he liked, he would recognize the song's potential immediately and say, "Hold it!" and play it over and over. The musicians would study the demo version along with Elvis and begin picking up the beats, riffs and chord changes, working up an arrangement. Elvis would often make suggestions to tailor the song to his desire, by altering the tempo, modifying a lyric, creating vocal background parts or embellishing the instrumentation. Like everything else, he conveyed his ideas instinctually…by using hand gestures, nodding, and making eye contact with the musicians, and they in turn read his expressions and followed his body language.

Some of my favorite memories are of watching Elvis at work in the recording studio. It was like witnessing a private Elvis concert. It was fascinating to observe the creative process and watch as Elvis and the band created classic hit records right before my eyes. When I hear an Elvis song on the radio, I tend to associate it with the session it was recorded at.

Elvis preferred to record his music live, in one continuous take, with the full band and background singers right there with him.

Certain instrumentation, like a stringed orchestra for example, would be added onto Elvis's completed take at a later session. These added musical performances are known as "overdubs". He did not like to just add his voice to pre-recorded backing tracks, and he did not like "punching in" individual lines or verses. Occasionally this was necessary, but 90% of every Elvis record you've ever heard is a straight ahead live performance. He liked to capture the spontaneity and "realness" of a live take and felt this technique, though more demanding, represented a more "honest" interpretation of the song. When selecting the final master, Elvis always deferred to the "feel" of the recording rather than it's technical consistency.

In the studio, Elvis would rarely just stand still in front of a stationary microphone and sing. He did on certain occasions, but more often than not he grasped onto a hand held mike and moved and gyrated amongst and between the various band members much like he did onstage during a concert. Sometimes this technique drove the producer and engineers crazy because the microphone was supposed to capture only Elvis's isolated vocal, so his voice could be blended and balanced with the instruments during the final mixing process. But the way Elvis liked to record, whenever he walked near any of the musicians, the microphone would pick up whatever instrument he was closest to and the music would "bleed" onto his vocal track. I remember one time Felton Jarvis was playing back some session tapes. Felton isolated Elvis's vocal track, and we could tell just by listening which musician he had been standing next to in the room based on which instrument faded in and out around his voice! Elvis also tended to "pop" the mike. In the heat of a live performance, his lips would sometimes get too close to the microphone and words starting with the "p" sound would make a "pop" noise. Once in 1973, Elvis recorded several songs right in the living room of his home in Palm Springs. There was no microphone stand in the house, so the guys fashioned one by sticking a mop into a wash bucket and duct taping the microphone to the mop handle. If you listen closely to some recordings, you can sometimes hear those "p" pops, among other extraneous studio sounds like rustling lyric pages, creaking stools, off-mike dialogue, or pieces of Elvis's jewelry clanking against the microphone!

After the success of his 1968 "Singer Presents Elvis" "comeback" TV special, Elvis took on a renewed interest in his music. For years his records had been limited mainly to songs written to suit specific scenes in his motion pictures. These movie songs have received a lot of flack from a majority of critics. But it's important to understand that these tunes served a specific purpose -- to further the plot of the films they appeared in. They were not meant to be compared commercially to the material on Elvis's mainstream albums. By similar example, "If I Only Had A Brain" is a wonderful number when heard within the fantasy context of "The Wizard of Oz", but it's not a song Shirley Bassey would choose to include in her concert repertoire. Songs like "Song Of The Shrimp" or "Queenie Wahine's Papaya" were tailored to fit on-screen situations and, to be fair, should be judged by a different standard than songs like "Hurt", "An American Trilogy", "For Ol' Times Sake" or "How Great Thou Art".

In most cases, the movie songs have gotten an undeserved bad rep. Sure, some of them were downright inferior, but those relatively few clunkers seem to have created the impression that all the movie songs were weak, which just isn't true. "Bossa Nova

Baby", "C'mon Everybody", "Jailhouse Rock", "Return To Sender", "Pocketful Of Rainbows", "A Little Less Conversation" and his signature tune, "Can't Help Falling In Love", are just a few examples of bona fide Elvis classics that emanated from his motion pictures.

The last time Elvis recorded in a conventional recording studio was in 1975. As I mentioned, after he turned forty, Elvis became much more withdrawn. I don't know why, but it became a struggle to get him into the studio to record new material. Elvis's contract with RCA dictated that a certain number of singles and LP albums had to be delivered per year. Felton Jarvis was forever sweating those deadlines. During the entire year 1974, Elvis did not enter a recording studio once. Record release schedules were accommodated by recording concerts ("Elvis As Recorded Live On Stage in Memphis") or by repackaging previously released material (" Pure Gold", "The Sun Sessions" the "A Legendary Performer" series). But by 1976, there was nothing new left to release! It was decided that since we couldn't get Elvis to the studio, we would bring the studio to Elvis. RCA soundproofed the den of Graceland, and a mobile recording truck was stationed outside. Audio cables were run from the truck into the house, and instruments and mikes were set up, effectively transforming Elvis's "jungle room", as it is now known, into a makeshift recording studio!

Now all Elvis had to do was leave his bed and walk down the stairs! Believe it or not, he would still keep the session waiting, sometimes for hours and hours! These Graceland sessions, taped during February and October of 1976, were the last "studio" recordings Elvis made during his lifetime. To prove he could still deliver the goods, consider that "For The Heart", "Pledging My Love", "Danny Boy", "Way Down", "Hurt" and "Moody Blue" were just some of the fine performances captured during these sessions. As I said in the 1981 documentary film, "This Is Elvis", "His incredible voice never failed him."

Speaking of "blue", it was during the session for "Hurt" that Elvis recorded a unique version of that song especially for his father. After completing the master take, he asked Felton and the band to run through the song one more time. When he reached the spoken part of his performance, Elvis twisted the lovelorn recitation into a shocking, X-rated verbal assault that would have made late 80's comedian Sam Kinnison blush! Once we all regained our composure, Elvis sent for his father, Vernon, and said, "Listen to this, Daddy. You'll love it". Felton ran the playback of "Hurt". The song's dramatic opening crescendo followed by Elvis's booming opening line blared through the speakers, filling the room with sound: "I'm...soooohuuuuurrt". Vernon listened intently to Elvis's impassioned, powerful vocal, nodding his approval. Moments later came the spoken second verse:

"I'm hurt...
much more...goddamnit honey,
I told you so...shit!...
yes darling, I'm so hurt...c***sucker!
Because...I still love you so...motherf***er!"

Vernon turned red. "Oh, lord have mercy, son...what am I gonna do with you?" he said, burying his face in his hands. It truly was one of the funniest pranks I've ever seen Elvis pull off. By the way, don't count on hearing this version of "Hurt" anytime soon. I believe Felton saw to it that tape was destroyed.

Most of the Graceland-recorded material was issued on the LP, "From Elvis Presley Boulevard, Memphis, Tennessee". There weren't many songs left over to release, and RCA needed more, particularly "rock" songs, for the next LP, designed to appeal to a younger, more contemporary audience. The general consensus among fans indicated they wanted this type of album too. For years Elvis had been leaning heavily towards performing dramatic, sentimental ballads and songs of unrequited love ("My Boy", "Fool", "Always On My Mind", "Pieces Of My Life"). Felton Jarvis really beat the bushes and found some excellent new up-tempo rock n' roll songs that he hand-picked especially for Elvis. He then booked session time at an up-and-coming studio known as "Creative Workshop", actually set up by songwriter and producer Buzz Cason within a small private home in Nashville. It was January 1977, shortly after Elvis's forty-second birthday; sadly, the Nashville sessions were never to materialize.

Elvis had only been dating Ginger Alden for about two months at the time, yet their relationship was already beginning to create frustration for him. Elvis was smitten with her to a fault. Ginger, however, was somewhat independent and aloof. She cared for Elvis in her own way, but catered more to the whims and needs of her family, especially her omnipresent mother. She didn't want to make the trip to Nashville with Elvis, and he was furious. He was accustomed to his women going dutifully along with what he decided, but Ginger consistently bucked him, and it made him crazy. Looking back, she lacked the maternal instincts, emotional maturity and blind dedication of his other girlfriends. To be fair, Ginger was young, only twenty, and less than half his age. She was understandably overwhelmed, thrust head first into Elvis's upside-down environment without any foretaste or awareness of exactly how stifling life with Elvis Presley could become. Ginger was torn between pleasing her family, meeting Elvis's demands and maintaining her own independent space. Strangely, the more Ginger resisted Elvis's amorous expectations, the more valiantly he fought to possess her. He couldn't seem to get this one under his thumb, and the fallout over this ongoing struggle effectively aborted the entire Nashville recording project.

Since Ginger refused to accompany him, Elvis arrived in Nashville predisposed with an ornery, negative mindset. As a result, he was in no shape to make music. We all sat at the hotel for days, waiting and waiting for Elvis's dark mood to lift. Felton and the entire crew were over at the studio waiting for us, laying down backing tracks for the scheduled tunes in order to make use of the session time. To be honest, Elvis could barely talk, let alone sing. He was totally "out of it". When Elvis got into a funk, like he was in this situation, he would just zone himself out. When he finally got himself together enough to make it over to the studio, we pulled up outside, and he took one look at it and said, "What the hell is this?" What we saw was just a small residential house. He hated the thought of it. He didn't need to travel to Nashville to record in someone else's house, and said, "If I'm going to record in a house, I'll record at Graceland." We turned around and that was it. The entire endeavor was for naught. This was another instance where the Colonel was rightfully upset. It was Elvis's responsibility to honor his recording commitments with the record label. The sad part was that Elvis never got around to recording all the great stuff Felton had planned for him.

Elvis never entered another recording studio again. In order to assemble what would become his final LP, "Moody Blue" (which, like it's predecessor contained only 10 songs), RCA had to utilize whatever was left from the Graceland sessions and pad the rest of the album out with several live tracks recorded during concerts later that spring.

As far as what Elvis's future with Ginger Alden might have been, I have my doubts that it would have continued on much longer. Although he impulsively held a private, mock engagement ceremony later that month at his home in Palm Springs (presided over by hairstylist Larry Geller), personally, I believe, it was more a manipulative ploy to conform and control her. Elvis would often say or do what he had to to get what he wanted. I'm sure if you asked Ginger, she would contend Elvis planned to marry her, and it's very likely that's what he said to her. But in private, Elvis candidly stated, "Ginger's on the way out." He was also growing increasingly wary of the Alden family's eager desire to reap the benefits of his reckless generosity. I distinctly recall plans were wavering on whether or not she would be accompanying him on the tour we were set to begin on August 17, so we had another girl lined up, waiting on standby, just in case.

We hope you have enjoyed part one... please join us for Volume 2 in the ELVIS-STRAIGHT UP series...

Available at:
www.elvisstraightup.com
and your nearest bookstore

A STEAMROLLER PUBLISHING PAPERBACK

We hope you will enjoy these other books from
TCB Joe Publishing

Remember Elvis

Produced by Joe Esposito

REMEMBER ELVIS is an all-encompassing, in-depth look at the life and career of a man whose popularity is unrivalled in the history of show business and who continues to attract millions of new fans each year.

This ground-breaking book is brimming with rare interviews, insights and experiences, previously unrevealed... until now.

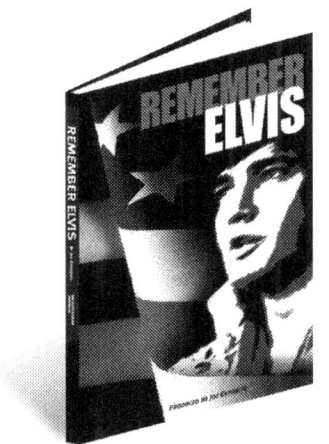

At the heart of this landmark project are over 200 interviews with many of Presley's most intimate associates, as well as some of the biggest names in the film and recording industries.

Available at:
www.rememberelvis.ca
and your nearest bookstore

Celebrate Elvis

Produced by Joe Esposito

Long-time Elvis insider and right hand man, Joe Esposito, lends his invaluable insights and memories to this exciting new series that will set you up and set you straight!

CELEBRATE ELVIS is just that... a celebration of Elvis's career, his life and his legacy. Loaded with fun stories, interviews, trivia and contributions from you, the fans.

CELEBRATE ELVIS is an uplifting, feel-good book that enlightens, entertains and informs!

Available at:
www.celebrateelvis.com
and your nearest bookstore

www.ingramcontent.com/pod-product-compliance
Lightning Source LLC
Chambersburg PA
CBHW080550170426
43195CB00016B/2735